CW00674739

Corporate Manslaughter in Maritime and Aviation Ind

Simon Daniels

Lloyd's Practical Shipping Guides

ISM Code: A Practical Guide to the Legal and Insurance Implications
Third Edition
Dr Phil Anderson
(2016)

Introduction to Marine Cargo Management
Second Edition
Mark Rowbotham
(2014)

Steel: Carriage by Sea
Fifth Edition
Arthur Sparks
(2010)

Port Operations: Planning and Logistics
Khalid Bichou
(2010)

Port Management and Operations
Third Edition
Professor Patrick M. Alderton
(2009)

Risk Management in Port Operations, Logistics and Supply Chain Security
Khalid Bichou, Michel G.H. Bell and Andrew Evans
(2008)

Maritime Law
Sixth Edition
Chris Hill
(2004)

Corporate Manslaughter in the Maritime and Aviation Industries

Simon Daniels

Routledge
Taylor & Francis Group

LONDON AND NEW YORK

First published 2017 by Informa Law from Routledge

2 Park Square, Milton Park, Abingdon, Oxfordshire OX14 4RN
52 Vanderbilt Avenue, New York, NY 10017

Routledge is an imprint of the Taylor & Francis Group, an informa business

First issued in paperback 2019

British Library Cataloguing in Publication Data
A catalogue record for this book is available from the British Library

Library of Congress Cataloging-in-Publication Data
A catalog record for this title has been requested

ISBN: 978-1-138-92047-7 (hbk)
ISBN: 978-0-367-87379-0 (pbk)

Typeset in Bembo
by Apex CoVantage, LLC

Contents

Author biography

Dr Simon Daniels is a solicitor of the Senior Courts of England and Wales, with many years' experience in criminal and civil litigation, most notably in international merchant shipping and civil aviation. While many of his cases involved the resolution of contract and commercial disputes, he enjoyed considerable diversity defending claims in negligence cases, and has advised in a number of criminal prosecutions in the maritime sphere.

In 1998 Simon diversified into commercial mediation as a Qualified Dispute Resolver and Member of the Faculty of Mediation and ADR, founded by the Academy of Experts in London, in furtherance of one of the Academy's principal objectives, the pursuit of cost-efficient dispute resolution. Simon was Secretary to the Academy between 2005 and 2009, and was one of the first commercial mediators who took part in the pilot mediation scheme in Central London County Court.

Simon has brought his professional background to the academic field, as Senior Lecturer in Maritime Law at Southampton Solent University, where he teaches in the Merchant Vessel Operations programme at Warsash Maritime Academy, one of the world's leading centres of excellence in training for merchant shipping professionals. In the wider academic field, he has written a number of papers on current law, in subjects with a particular focus on corporate accountability both in domestic and international contexts.

Simon has a particular interest in the field of the criminalisation of the ship's master, which harnesses his professional career to his background in the maritime industry and in 2012 was awarded a PhD for his thesis: *The Criminalisation of the Ship's Master. A new approach for the new millennium.*

In October 2005, Simon was admitted to Freedom of the Worshipful Company of Arbitrators. In 2006 he was made a Freeman By Redemption of the City of London.

Table of cases

Table of legislation

1   Introduction

1.1 Justice or criminalisation? The fundamentals of accountability for manslaughter in the maritime and civil aviation industries

In his paper 'The Homicide Ladder' in the *Modern Law Review*,[1] Victor Tadros states:

> *When death is caused it is a natural reaction to look around for someone to blame . . . The fact that our intuitions in attributing blame for death tend not to track the wrongfulness of the killing very accurately provides a powerful reason for the law to differentiate between degrees of wrongdoing more precisely. In distinguishing between different levels of wrongdoing, the law provides public guidance about how we should perceive the killer where it is needed most, where our intuitions, particularly if we are bound up with the deceased, often fail us.*

The wrongdoing of manslaughter has historically proved especially troublesome to establish with clarity, as described famously by Lord Atkin in *Andrews v DPP*:[2]

> *Of all crimes manslaughter appears to afford most difficulties of definition, for it concerns homicide in so many and so varying conditions . . . the law . . . recognises murder on the one hand based mainly, though not exclusively, on an intention to kill, and manslaughter on the other hand, based mainly, but not exclusively, on the absence of intent to kill, but with the presence of an element of 'unlawfulness' which is the elusive factor.*

Corporate accountability does not lend itself to precise definition, but has been well summarised by Swift as addressing the requirement or duty to provide an

---

1   Tadros, V, (2006) 69(4) MLR 601–618, at 601.
2   *Andrews v DPP* [1937] 2 All ER 552 (at pp554–555).

account or justification for one's actions to whomever one is answerable.[3] The 'whomever' has come to be known as the stakeholder; just who satisfies that definition naturally has been the subject of litigation in negligence for generations, but the neighbour principle in *Donoghue v Stevenson* must offer the best guidance in the context of this work: a stakeholder will be somebody so closely and directly affected by the company's act that it should reasonably foresee that they would be so affected.[4] With the implementation of the Corporate Manslaughter and Corporate Homicide Act 2007, corporate accountability for the crime of manslaughter has taken on statutory form, which satisfies the normative ethics of a society that demands redress for catastrophic events such as the *Herald of Free Enterprise* and the *Marchioness* disasters but at the cost of the nerves of ship operators. This chapter charts the decline and fall of the relationship, culminating in a study of the issues for combating piracy – the current event that might just make or break the relationship.

1.2 The risk society

The society that moulds our laws and standards never stands still. The nineteenth century ethic that focused on economic inequality has subtly changed priority, to public safety, whether that be life or the environment. Globally we have already seen the rise of this risk society, which goes to the core of the grievance that may be harboured by people when confronted with the ultimate risk, of a fatal accident. It is not just an issue between members of society within a single state, but also those who have a grievance against those who may be governed by the laws of another state, whose laws may be punitive towards foreign nationals, but effective, just the same – in other words, where the laws of a sovereign jurisdiction clash with the rights and obligations of other ships, or other aircraft, and the people who manage them.

The approach taken to legislation by a risk society presents a clear tension that has a dynamic on the definition of a moral wrong in the context of normative ethics. The underlying causes of this tension may be identified in terms of a concern for the safety of the individual, for the environment and for the state.[5] Such conflicting issues in this tension compel the risk society to practise the judgement of Solomon, and trade off the merits of ethical arguments that may place the individual and the state on a collision course. For the judgement to demonstrate that it has met the fundamental demands of justice, the risk society has to make decisions that must strike a balance between the regula-

3   Swift, T, *Business Ethics: A European Review*, Vol 10, No 1, January 2001, Blackwell Publishers Ltd, London, pp16–26.
4   *Donoghue (or McAlister) v Stevenson* [1932] All ER Rep 1; [1932] AC 562.
5   Hudson, B, 2003, *Justice in the Risk Society*, Sage, London, p203ff.

tion of criminal activity by the restraint of punishment, and the respect and maintenance of limits on such punishment. Inevitably the clash comes when the judgment must confront the seemingly intractable problem of rationalising and justifying the argument for deciding what human rights should be suspended in the interests of the sovereign state in question. Put in context, this challenges society to convey a compelling decision to make the master of a ship or the pilot in command of an aircraft accountable for wrongs that the risk society perceives itself to have suffered – simply because of the fact of the responsibility of the master or the pilot in command, rather than the presence of any characteristics of a crime. For the company that owns the ship, or the aircraft, herein lies the very real threat to its rights to peaceful operation.

The shipowner identifies a very real danger with the evolution of the law of criminal negligence against the master, should the master incriminate them in a crime under the new Corporate Manslaughter Act,[6] whose origins stemmed from public and political unhappiness with the corporate positions presented in the *Herald of Free Enterprise* and *Marchioness* disasters, among others. The offence is committed if the way in which the company's activities are managed or organised causes a person's death, and amounts to a gross breach of a relevant duty of care owed by the organisation to the deceased. Liability for the death no longer must be attributed to the conviction of manslaughter against a member of the controlling mind of the company, but by a 'management failure' involving a person who plays a significant role in the making of decisions about how the activities are to be managed or organised, or the actual managing or organising of the whole or a substantial part of those activities. The master fits perfectly this definition. If a person is killed, and particularly if the master is confronted with allegations of criminal negligence, that may be used in evidence against their employer, the shipowner, in order to establish that there was a management failure giving rise to the crime of corporate manslaughter. The UK Government's Sentencing Council[7] published guidelines which were updated in 2015, providing that the fine which would likely be imposed upon the convicted company would be within a range of £180,000 to £20 million.

Such threats encourage the owner to distance themselves from the master as far as they possibly can, for, if the owner is to be held vicariously liable for gross negligence then the consequences in terms of damages may result in punishment which the maritime world had seen first imposed in *the Exxon Valdez*

---

6   Section 1 of the Corporate Manslaughter and Corporate Homicide Act 2007: An organisation to which this section applies is guilty of an offence if the way in which its activities are managed or organised causes a person's death and amounts to a gross breach of a relevant duty of care owed by the organisation to the deceased.

7   www.sentencingcouncil.org.uk/wp-content/uploads/HS-offences-definitive-guideline-FINAL-web.pdf.

case for the pollution of the marine environment, involving fines, punishing compensation claims, and plunging share values with which to contend. This translates all too easily to the scenario in which the gross negligence has given rise to a fatal accident. No better example can be found than in the *Costa Concordia* casualty, in which the corporate share value plunged after the event, and recovered after the master was convicted without due criminal process attending the owner; or the case of Malaysian Airlines, whose prosperity was extinguished in the wake of the MH370 and MH17 disasters.

It is as well, therefore, to start a review of corporate manslaughter by examining the bottom line – the accountability of those key individuals with senior management control whose decisions, likely taken in the heat of the moment, lead to the company's arraignment. And at the heart of the controversy, is the mischief of the master's criminalisation.

The first thing to consider is just what is defined as a crime. The case of *Shaw v DPP*[8] still holds good:

> *There remains in the Courts of Law a residual power to enforce the supreme and fundamental purpose of the law, to conserve not only the safety and order but also the moral welfare of the State, and that it is their duty to guard it against attacks which may be the more insidious because they are novel and unprepared for*[9]

1.3 How has this affected the master?

The master has undergone a process by which their responsibility to manage a maritime risk has been opened up to ever-growing accountability to the criminal law as society sees new threats to its welfare, caused by the very hazards that the beleaguered master is trying to avoid.

To understand the phenomenon, we need to understand some history in the master's management of risk, for which we have a perfect example in UK–China trade.

Captain Arthur Clark[10] summed up the business of maritime trade when he observed that the demand for tea in the mid-nineteenth century created a breed of master who could deliver their cargoes to the tea auctions in London as rapidly as possible, in order to fetch the highest price. Speeds of 16 knots by these extreme clippers were regularly achieved, and Lyon reported 12 instances of clippers logging 18 knots and over[11] and, while *Cutty Sark* had a top speed

---

8 *Shaw v Director of Public Prosecutions* [1962] AC 220, [1961] UKHL 1, [1961] 2 All ER 446, (1961) 45 Cr App R 113.
9 Per Viscount Simonds.
10 Clark, A, 1910, *The Clipper Ship Era*, G E Putnam's Sons, New York.
11 Lyon, J, 1962, *Clipper Ships and Captains*, American Heritage Publishing, New York, p138.

exceeding 17 knots[12] she once achieved an *average* of 15 knots.[13] But the risk was high. It was still an era in which the naval architecture of a merchant ship was a study in trial and error, making it necessary for the owners to repose all their confidence in the master's professional skill and judgement in order to avoid disaster. In the words of American Professor John Augustus Shedd:

> *A ship in harbor is safe, but that is not what ships are built for.*[14]

Given that maritime technology was positively embryonic, the very fact of the season's weather that the clippers had to endure demanded great skill in the design of the new ships, which invariably had to sail home from China while the southwest monsoon was still raging.[15]

The successful master was the one who conducted a risk–benefit analysis designed to maximise the commercial return, and mitigate the dangers if possible. His job had but one objective: to make a fast passage, and the master had a vested interest in securing a full hold of cargo, for he was able to draw a percentage of the freight that was earned. A successful master could earn the enormous sum of £5,000 a year,[16] and so he drove his ship to the limits of her endurance, slashing home through the English Channel, a hundred days out of China. Some masters only went below to change their clothes or take a bath; others used the settee in the chart room or even a deck-chair as a bed.

Far from criminalising the master for their reckless disregard of risk, society actually applauded it. From the traders in the City of London, who had a sporting interest in backing their investment, to the locals in the humblest village inn, bets were placed and arguments raged over the favoured contenders. In the great race of 1866, the crews of the *Serica* and *Fiery Cross* bet a month's pay against each other that they would be first home to London.

12 In 1889, she was involved in a famous incident with P&O's crack, two-year old, state-of-the-art steamship *Britannia* when, on the night of 25 July, *Britannia*, doing between 14.5 and 16 knots, was overhauled by *Cutty Sark* doing a good 17 knots. Robert Olivey, Second Officer on *Britannia*, watched the lights of the sailing ship overhauling his vessel with amazement and called Captain Hector. In fact they did not appreciate that it was *Cutty Sark*, and *Britannia*'s log read with great amazement, '*Sailing ship overhauled and passed us!*'.

13 By remarkable contrast, the cutting-edge, twenty-first century generation of bulk carriers ordered by the China Navigation Company of the Swire Group are designed for a speed of 14 knots. See www.swire.com/en/our-businesses/marine-services/shipping-lines/swire-bulk.

14 Quoted by Shapiro, F, 2006, *The Yale Book of Quotations*, Yale University Press, New Haven, p705.

15 '*they had to be smart in moderate weather going to windward, as well as in getting through the northeast trades in the Atlantic. It was under these conditions that they did their best work. They did not carry as heavy spars nor as much canvas as the American clippers of the same length, and probably could not have done so to advantage, as their breadth was considerably less, and with their easy lines they did not require much canvas to drive them*': Clark, A, supra, p321.

16 Approximately £445,000 in 2015; by comparison, the master of a dry bulk carrier in the same trade today would expect to receive a salary between £60,000 and £80,000.

Not a voice was raised against the masters who took risks that, today, might give rise to accusations of gross negligence. It is to their credit that, of the entire list of great contenders only ten clippers were wrecked on the China tea passages,[17] the *Lahloo* famously being among them. Captain John Smith had commanded her since her maiden voyage and in the words of MacGregor *drove her hard all the time.* She was wrecked on 31 July 1872,[18] through the alleged fault of her second mate, who, under the stress and pressure of a hard voyage, piled her up on Sandalwood Island, one of the Sunda Islands in the Malay archipelago.[19] It was, of course, a disaster but no lives were lost and even part of the cargo was saved, much to the delight of the stakeholders. Far from suffering any legal or professional consequence, Captain Smith was appointed by the owners, Killick Martin, to supervise the construction of their new tea clipper at Dundee.[20] There was no question of an inquiry into anybody's criminal accountability.

The master was accountable under the criminal law generally in the same way as any subject would be; but society was more discerning about his account-ability as master under God, which is well illustrated in the dramatic case of *Regina v Dudley and Stephens.*[21] On 5 July 1884 Tom Dudley, skipper of the yacht *Mignonette,* abandoned the sinking vessel with his three crew, who drifted helplessly in their lifeboat for 20 days, before he made the command decision to sacrifice the cabin boy so that the others might remain alive long enough to be saved. Having killed him they planned to live on the remains until they were rescued. After they were brought back to England, Dudley was tried and convicted of murder; but the normative ethics of society of the day was outraged by the verdict and the Home Secretary bowed to the demand of the electorate with a pardon for the defendants.

1.4 So what has changed?

It is still the normative ethics of society which determines criminal account-ability, and the society of the twenty-first century has drawn very different opinions on criminalisation in shipping and aviation for acts that previously had not been crimes.

The foundation of this corporate accountability lies in the basic idea of an innocent approach taken by the company – or, rather, by senior managers in that company who have the power to protect or to harm. As a result, we start from

---

17 MacGregor, D, 1952, *The Tea Clippers*, Conway Maritime Press and Lloyd's of London Press.
18 *Ariel*, winner of the great race of 1866, was lost without trace on a voyage from London to Sydney in 1872.
19 Lubbock, B, 1914, *The China Clippers*, Brown Son & Ferguson Ltd, p217, who gave the date as 30th.
20 The *Maju* sailed on her maiden voyage under the command of Captain Smith, but was then lost with all hands in a great storm five days later.
21 *R v Dudley and Stephens* (1884) 14 QBD 273 DC.

the position that only on rare occasions will hardworking and inherently honest humans knowingly commit an act of wrongdoing. In most cases the person merely makes an assumption in the risk management exercise that only achieves significance later on. Examples of such innocent assumptions may include:

- *Everybody does it.* In other words, if it is common practice, then they cannot be blamed for a fatal result.
- *It's no big deal.* A risk assessment would lead to the conclusion that it could be tolerated on account of its likely minor consequence.
- *The problem will go away.* If the risk is tolerated, then it will shrink to something below what society would deem blameworthy.

But society has given fresh thought to the ethics that it expects of business in balancing commercial risk against health and safety. We can summarise this with a non-marine illustration that leads us to challenge corporate accountability from the viewpoint of society.

In the lean years of the 1970s the Ford Motor Company wanted to break into the economy car market, and developed the Pinto. It was only after the development project had been completed that the board were warned of a major problem with the vehicle's fuel system, which could lead to death or serious personal injury. Ford undertook a cost–benefit analysis, in which it was revealed that safety design options would cost between $1.80 and $15.30 per Pinto, totalling $137 million per year; whereas civil claims of $200,000 per death, $67,000 per injury, $700 per vehicle would total some $49.5 million. In the light of this, Ford proceeded to take the risk.

Thirteen-year-old Richard Grimshaw received horrific injuries in 1972 when he was travelling as a passenger in a Pinto when it was involved in a rear-end collision in which it became an inferno. In subsequent proceedings[22] the California jury set punitive damages against Ford of $126 million for Richard Grimshaw, setting a benchmark for punitive damages awards, and only in a recent case has there been a refined definition of punitive damages to reduce the total quantum in claims arising out of such reckless disregard for human life.[23]

Shortly following the Grimshaw verdict, Ford faced criminal proceedings arising out of another Ford Pinto tragedy when, in 1978, three teenage girls driving in a Ford Pinto were hit from behind on Highway 33 in northern Indiana. Within moments their car burst into flames and all three of the girls were killed. An Indiana grand jury voted unanimously to indict Ford Motor Company on three counts of homicide, for recklessly designing, manufacturing and marketing the Pinto's unsafe fuel tank, in part because the corporation was

---

22   *Grimshaw v Ford Motor Co* (1981) 119 Cal App 3d 757.
23   *State Farm Automobile Ins Co v Campbell*, 538 US 31 PSLR 321 (2003).

aware of the design defects of the Pinto before production but did not rectify the problems.

The final verdict was not guilty,[24] but the lesson learned was that corporations can be charged with criminal homicide in United States' courts. American criminal law has a close affinity with English criminal law, opening the door to a new era in corporate accountability for manslaughter. All it took, was for some gross negligent manslaughter to take place by an individual and that such an act could be traced back to the controlling mind of the company – such an individual might be the master, or the pilot in command.

And the normative ethics in this new risk society demanded somebody to blame. In the United States and in the United Kingdom, the principles of integrity and justice are guarded jealously and upheld proudly; in many other states, though, this may not be the first priority. It is the inescapable truth of the criminalisation phenomenon, that, if the defendant is arraigned, tried and sentenced within the judicial process of a sovereign state, the law, for better or for worse, has taken its course, and it is this tension between justice and fairness that has brought the topic of criminalisation to the top of the maritime agenda. The position in law underlines the tension between port and coastal states on one side and flag states on the other, focusing on the interpretation by such states of their sovereign authority to enforce their society's approach to the characteristics of a moral wrong and how that must interface with their international obligations to convention partners such as flag states. The court in any democracy, after all, is bound by the constitutional parameters of its powers, which have been accorded to it by the state, that is, by its own people in a democratic system.

Against this background, let us set in context the evolution of corporate accountability under English law, which will enable us to understand where the present law is going.

---

24   *State of Indiana v Ford Motor Co*, Cause No 11–431 (1980).

2 Examining the bottom line

A comparative study of the key players

2.1 The accountability of the master

The master has always been subject to the law of the flag state. In law, his is the ultimate authority for the vessel over which he has sole command and he is responsible to the flag state for compliance with all its laws, for his authority and accountability are derived primarily from the laws of the flag state. So what are the flag state's obligations?

The state is primarily obliged to meet its treaty obligations with other signatories; in context this takes us to the United Nations Convention on the Law of the Sea[1] (UNCLOS), which defines the critical issues of sovereignty and the associated jurisdiction over ships of whatever flag. The convention preserves the sovereign jurisdiction of flag states over their ships wherever they are in the world, limiting the coastal state's sovereign jurisdiction subject to the right of ships of all states to '*innocent passage through the territorial sea*'.[2]

This underlines the overarching principle that the ship is, in law, very much a piece of sovereign territory of the state in which she is registered, and will be controlled and regulated by that state's laws, of whatever sort, wherever she may be in the world. Article 87 enshrines the ancient doctrine of the freedom of the high seas outside the territorial sea:[3]

> *The high seas are open to all States, whether coastal or land-locked. Freedom of the high seas is exercised under the conditions laid down by this Convention and by other rules of international law. It comprises, inter alia. . . freedom of navigation; . . . freedom of overflight;*

Article 2, however, assures the coastal state its sovereign jurisdiction, to the exclusion of other states, from its land territory to an adjacent belt of sea, described in

1 United Nations Convention on the Law of the Sea, signed in 1982, replacing four 1958 treaties. UNCLOS came into force in 1994. As of January 2015, 166 countries have signed the convention.
2 Article 17.
3 And the exclusive economic zone, over which the coastal state does not enjoy sovereign jurisdiction save for the protection of resources.

Article 3 as the territorial sea '*up to a limit not exceeding 12 nautical miles, measured from baselines. . . .*'

Article 2 further assures a state its sovereignty to the air space over the territorial sea as well as to its bed and subsoil.

So what if there were to be some jurisdictional conflict between flag state and coastal state in terms of criminal jurisdiction? UNCLOS clearly must determine the applicable regulation in a coastal state's sovereign jurisdiction:[4]

1   *The criminal jurisdiction of the coastal State should not be exercised on board a foreign ship passing through the territorial sea to arrest any person or to conduct any investigation in connection with any crime committed on board the ship during its passage, save only in the following cases:*

   (a)   *if the consequences of the crime extend to the coastal State;*
   (b)   *if the crime is of a kind to disturb the peace of the country or the good order of the territorial sea;*
   (c)   *if the assistance of the local authorities has been requested by the master of the ship or by a diplomatic agent or consular officer of the flag State; or*
   (d)   *if such measures are necessary for the suppression of illicit traffic in narcotic drugs or psychotropic substances.*

As a result, the very fact that the master assented to the process of certification by the authority of the flag state makes out an unassailable argument that he has voluntarily subjected himself to all the laws of the flag state and, necessarily, the applicable laws of a port state in whose sovereign jurisdiction he has voluntarily entered.

The master's accountability for the safe navigation of the vessel is derived from SOLAS[5] Ch V regulation 34:

1   *Prior to proceeding to sea, the master shall ensure that the intended voyage has been planned using the appropriate nautical charts and nautical publications for the area concerned, taking into account the guidelines and recommendations developed by the Organization.*
2   *The voyage plan shall identify a route which:*

   2.1   *takes into account any relevant ships' routeing systems*
   2.2   *ensures sufficient sea room for the safe passage of the ship throughout the voyage*
   2.3   *anticipates all known navigational hazards and adverse weather conditions; and*
   2.4   *takes into account the marine environmental protection measures that apply, and avoids, as far as possible, actions and activities which could cause damage to the environment*

---

4   Article 27.
5   International Convention for the Safety of Life at Sea, 1974 as amended.

But he retains absolute discretion, in a rule far predating any international convention but enshrined in SOLAS V regulation 34–1:

> *The owner, the charterer, the company operating the ship as defined in regulation IX/1, or any other person shall not prevent or restrict the master of the ship from taking or executing any decision which, in the master's professional judgement, is necessary for safety of life at sea and protection of the marine environment.*

So, to sum up the master's responsibility, while he retains absolute discretion, he remains accountable for his command decisions. In his judgment in *Grace v General Steam Navigation Company*,[6] a civil case involving an allegation of negligence on the part of the master, Mr Justice Devlin famously expressed his sympathies with the master, whose professional judgement on all the factors determining safety must be exercised at the time when the master makes his decision to proceed. While he must anticipate situations as part of his risk-management function, the master is not expected to be clairvoyant. As a result, his professional judgement will be based on factors such as the estimated position that would be reached at the planned time by any well-informed and experienced master; if a decision is based upon such an estimate the master's culpability will not be affected by the fact that, in the light of subsequent events, it is proved to be erroneous. At most that would be a mere error of judgement, which does not itself give rise to liability in negligence, which is dependent upon a wrong done and an injury actually sustained, giving rise to a right to damages; that right does not, by itself, follow someone's estimate of whether a wrong is likely to be done or an injury likely to be sustained. As Justice Devlin concluded:

> *A Master is not to be deprived of his remedy because, in ignorance of the danger, he entered a port which well-informed men might have erroneously pronounced his entry into the port to be foolhardy.*[7]

The question in this case depended upon the master's own judgement – it must be established that the standard of care reasonably owed by the master as a professional person has been broken. Historic authority for distancing the idea of a mere error of judgement from liability for negligence is found in the British Wreck Commissioner's Inquiry into the *Titanic* disaster, in which Sir Robert Finlay, representing the White Star Line, invited the court to find that there was

---

6   *G W Grace & Company Ltd v General Steam Navigation Company Limited* [1950] 2 KB 383.
7   Ibid, p394.

not even a mere error of judgement on the part of the navigating officers, to which the Wreck Commissioner, Lord Mersey, said:

> *That means also no negligence.*

Sir Robert Finlay replied, '*Certainly*'.[8]

The picture in current law has evolved more clearly still, to shed much light on the standards by which an allegation of negligence must be tested. This is conveyed articulately in the more recent case of *Passarello v Grumbine*[9] in the Superior Court of Pennsylvania, which establishes key principles for us, and clarifies the issue well that, in cases in which the judgement of a professional person is concerned, negligence cannot be established merely because of an unfortunate result that might have occurred despite the exercise of reasonable care. This case involved a claim in negligence against a physician but the rule applies equally to masters that such professional persons are permitted a broad range of judgement when carrying out their professional duties and so are not liable for errors of judgement unless it has been proved that an error of judgement was the result of negligence. Crucially for the case of the master, it was held that the standard of care to be established in professional negligence cases is objective in nature, because it focuses on the knowledge, skill, and care normally possessed and exercised by the professional in question. Consideration of a mere 'error of judgement' improperly refocuses attention on the professional's state of mind at the time; it is improper because the civil tort of negligence is concerned with consequences, a test that must be objective, rather than the defendant's state of mind that determines his guilt of a crime, which must be established by a subjective test.

This underscores one of the critical problem areas which define the ills of criminalisation, for the evolution of modern criminal liability owes a great deal to the civil tort of negligence. The downstream consequence is that the characteristics of certain crimes, to which the master has been exposed in recent times, have had to evolve in reliance upon the civil tort of negligence in order to meet social demands for the criminalisation of the master's professional activity; *Passarello v Grumbine* homes in on the key point, that the respective objective and subjective tests for establishing liability are irreconcilable and render the idea of criminal negligence fatally flawed.

---

8   British Wreck Commissioner's Inquiry, 'Report on the Loss of the "Titanic" (SS)' (30 July 1912), Day 28.

9   *Steven P Passarello and Others v Rowena T Grumbine and Others*, No 1399 WDA 2010; 2011 PA Super 199.

2.2 The case of Captain Mangouras

The normative ethics of society will not be denied. While observing those ethics, the task of risk management by the port state clearly demands the strict observance of the master's human rights during the litigation process – the right to a fair trial has long preceded written international conventions.[10] That being said, an uncomfortably large percentage of cases illustrates the delicate balance to be struck between the administration of justice and the will of the people, which may not always be harmonious. A glaring example of this is found in the case of Captain Mangouras, master of the *Prestige*, which, in November 2002, was involved in a catastrophic event that led to a spill of 70,000 tonnes of fuel oil into the sea, endangering marine life and, consequently, leading to a criminal investigation by the Spanish authorities. In the meantime, the Spanish court remanded Captain Mangouras, a Greek national, in custody and set his bail at an incredible 3 million euros. The case was appealed to the European Court of Human Rights on the grounds of an infringement of the European Convention on Human Rights.[11]

The European Court confirmed[12] that a remand in custody with such a high bail could only be required as long as reasons justifying that detention prevailed, and that the authorities had to take as much care in fixing appropriate bail as in deciding whether or not the defendant's continued detention was indispensable. But the court went on to uphold the normative ethics of the port state over the human rights of the master and expressed the opinion that new realities had to be taken into consideration in interpreting the requirements of the Human Rights Convention, namely what it referred to as '*the growing and legitimate concern both in Europe and internationally in relation to environmental offences and the tendency to use criminal law as a means of enforcing the environmental obligations imposed by European and international law*'.[13] The court held the view that the increasingly high standard that was demanded by individual human rights required greater firmness in assessing breaches of the fundamental values of democratic societies. In consequence, the court could not rule out the professional environment that made demands upon a master in Captain Mangouras's position. The court went further and approved the relevance of the environmental damage in considering the question, and expressed no surprise that the Spanish court should have adjusted the amount required by way of bail in line with the level of liability incurred. The master was in custody for 83 days before a bank guarantee for the

---

10 Magna Carta 1215 (final amendment 1225) 'No free man shall be seized or imprisoned, or stripped of his rights or possessions except by the lawful judgement of his peers' and 'To no one will we sell, to no one deny or delay right or justice.'

11 Articles 3 and 5 (security and liberty).

12 *Mangouras v Spain* (12050/04).

13 The author's reading of the text of the Judgment, which is in French.

sum was arranged, not by Captain Mangouras's owners, but by the protection and indemnity insurers. Given the trending accountability of the company for what a court considers to be their master's crimes, an accompanying trend by the company to distance itself from a master who is confronted by a prosecution for such a crime is, at least, understandable.

While Article 194(1) UNCLOS categorically clothes the port state, as any other, with the authority to take all measures (which, at least, are consistent with the convention) to prevent, reduce and control pollution of the marine environment, Professor Mukherjee[14] points out that the port state is not permitted to imprison a master for polluting the marine environment except where wilful and serious negligence has been proved. Article 230(2) of UNCLOS, the relevant provision, specifically qualifies the port state's enforcement rights against foreign *vessels*[15] by permitting only fines to be imposed by its courts against foreign flag vessels where there have been breaches of its domestic laws or applicable international rules and standards, and, further, the port state is obliged to observe the accused's rights under subsection (3). That being said, the decision of the European Court of Human Rights in *Mangouras v Spain* has a chilling note on the approach to the criminalisation of the master, even in the context of their own human rights:

> *The Court could not disregard the growing and legitimate concern both in Europe and internationally about offences against the environment. It noted in that connection the States' powers and obligations regarding the prevention of marine pollution and the unanimous determination among States and European and international organisations to identify those responsible, to ensure that they appeared to stand trial and to punish them.*[16]

Many would say that the effect of the decision in *Intertanko*[17] leaves port states with the comfortable illusion that they could justify criminal regulation of the master under European law even if it is inconsistent with the body of international law, which should, in fact, prevail. The decision in the *Mangouras* case only serves to perpetuate the illusion and, as an inevitable consequence, sets port states on a collision course with flag states, with the master in the middle and their company, the shipowner, vicariously liable for criminal negligence, which

---

14 Mukherjee, P, 2006, 'Criminalisation and Unfair Treatment: The seafarer's Perspective', *Journal of International Maritime Law*, Vol 12.

15 The Convention's word in italics; it is noteworthy that the employment of the words 'vessel' and 'accused' in this provision may lead to broad interpretations by the port state's prosecutor as to whom they may regard as the offender.

16 *Mangouras v Spain* (12050/04); para 3 Summary of Judgment.

17 *R (on the application of International Association of Independent Tanker Owners (Intertanko) and others) v Secretary of State for Transport* (Case C-308/06).

is why it is such a critical issue in this work. The conclusion must be drawn that the administration of justice in the context of European law exposes it to a clash of irreconcilable differences with key elements of legal theory, concisely summed up by the Law Commission in its 2010 consultation paper:

> *The criminal law. . . should not be used as the primary means of promoting regulatory objectives.*[18]

Just how a reconciliation can be made between the two remains a challenge.

Mention has been made of Intertanko, which is an independent association of tanker owners and operators with a professed vision of '*a professional, efficient and respected industry that is dedicated to achieving safe transport, cleaner seas and free competition*'.[19] It has repeatedly struck a lead in cases in defence of the master facing criminalisation[20] but the most recent decision in the case of Captain Mangouras deserves particular attention. The key issue surrounds the lesser charge on which he was convicted, in which the court chose to apply a political approach to two foundations of international maritime law; yet, they were acting within their sovereign jurisdiction, and they had the European Court decision to back them up.

In January 2016, the Spanish Supreme Court bizarrely reversed what had confidently been expected as the final issue of the case, and held Captain Mangouras guilty of gross negligence in his professional judgement for the safe navigation of his ship after she became imperilled by storm damage. In 2013 the lower court found Captain Mangouras not guilty of criminal negligence but that he was liable for disobedience of the Spanish authorities during the incident. The court held that this offence had not contributed to environmental damage, though. Captain Mangouras was sentenced to nine months in prison all the same. As this alleged disobedience was not causative of the damage, the court was not able to award compensation to the Spanish authorities. The court now changed its mind and decided that his conduct caused catastrophic environmental damage. The inconsistency inevitably raises questions about the Spanish court's motivation to establish grounds for recovering damages during the country's current financial crisis, which appears to outweigh the interests of justice considered by the lower court, surely the only basis upon which the process of a sovereign state should proceed.

18 Law Commission, 2010, 'Criminal Liability in Regulatory Contexts', Consultation Paper No 195, HMG, London, paragraph 1.28.

19 See www.intertanko.com.

20 See *R (on the application of International Association of Independent Tanker Owners (Intertanko) and others) v Secretary of State for Transport* supra.

The consequence of the Spanish court's decision is far more likely to involve consequences that go beyond the suspected motive of financial gain, and will have far-reaching effects on the confidence of other states in the trust and reliability of the Spanish legal process. But all it can do is to increase the tension between states, because, like it or not, the decision by the Supreme Court was made in the judicial process of a sovereign state, and no other state can interfere in that.

Mention has been made of the master's absolute discretion in discharging his flag state responsibilities under SOLAS,[21] which perpetuates the provisions that formerly defined the master's absolute discretion since the days of common law, in that nobody – not the owner, the charterer, or any other person – shall have the power to override the master's professional judgement in taking a decision that is necessary for the safety of life at sea and protection of the marine environment. That does not mean that the master shall not be accountable, but it shall be for the master to decide and, if he initially refuses to be towed back out to sea, as Captain Mangouras did, then the coastal state would have to convey a very compelling argument indeed that the master exercised his discretion to the detriment of his flag state responsibilities. It is submitted that it would be wholly unsafe to allow a court to apply a political decision that overrode the master's flag state responsibilities.

Nevertheless, Captain Mangouras was convicted of a criminal offence, carrying a term of imprisonment, for disobedience of the Spanish coastal state instruction to put back to sea with his stricken ship to face an oncoming storm with no specific destination, even though he was diligently discharging his flag state responsibilities. There cannot be any doubt that the Spanish coastal state instruction was made to serve the political demands of the Spanish community and the state itself. The criminalisation element flagrantly disregards the spirit of MARPOL,[22] which makes a strict liability offence of a pollution event in the coastal state's waters and, by the same token, gives the master a due diligence defence, which need only be proved on the civil burden of the balance of probabilities that he could not reasonably have done more in the discharge of his flag state duties. Even if that were established, UNCLOS provides for monetary penalties only for a pollution offence except in the case of a wilful and serious act of pollution in the territorial sea – again, hardly an issue when the master is exercising his flag state duties.

To set this in the context of this case, it is noteworthy that Captain Mangouras had stayed on board the vessel at great risk to his own safety; indeed, Intertanko made the astute observation that '*he had courageously done everything possible to*

---

21 SOLAS Ch V Regulation 34–1 supra.
22 International Convention for the Prevention of Pollution from Ships 1973/1978 as amended.

*protect crew, ship and cargo and to protect the environment by minimizing pollution –
including remaining on board. . . after the rest of the crew had been evacuated, in order to
try and save the ship'.*[23]

English law embraces a maxim that not only must justice be done, but must
be seen to be done,[24] which necessarily precludes any political bias in making
a judgment; and, as if the conviction and sentence of Captain Mangouras were
not bad enough, the maxim entirely discredits the court's acquittal of José Luis
López Sors González, the former head of Spain's merchant marine department
who had refused to allow the vessel to seek a place of refuge, thus sending the
vessel out to face an oncoming storm with no specific destination. The consequence of González's acquittal, however, conveniently meant that the Spanish
state would not be held responsible for the disaster.

In these circumstances, every sympathy may be held with the conclusion of
Intertanko that the Spanish judgment set a precedent that could only perpetuate and exacerbate master's criminalisation, for which the shipowner will be
vicariously liable, even though the master will have used their best endeavours
to mitigate loss and meet their flag state obligations to the safety of life at sea.
The downstream consequence is that political priorities are likely to underpin
the criminal process, and international law does nothing to undermine that.
Captain Mangouras was lucky to have been acquitted of more severe criminal
charges, and then unlucky enough to have the acquittal reversed on appeal, but
such accountability has developed in recent years, which characterises the modern phenomenon of criminalisation, to which the master is exposed when they
have to manage the business of risk, and this accountability has been identified
with the strange, hybrid features of criminal negligence.

The advantage to the state prosecutor of criminal negligence is that it need
not be necessary to establish a guilty mind in order to secure a conviction. Smith
and Hogan view with dismay the recent history of criminal convictions in the
English system with the observation that there has been a disproportionate use
of the criminal law to deal with regulatory offences.[25] A strict liability offence
is, by its nature, a regulatory offence, for mens rea is not required in establishing
liability. As a result, the development of prosecutions for criminal negligence
against the master may satisfy the normative ethics of society by levelling criminal blame for a regulatory offence, but that does not make it right. When
applied in context, we see the master being arraigned on charges of criminal
accountability for the consequences of what may merely have been negligence
in the eyes of civil law.

---

23 See www.intertanko.com.
24 *R v Sussex Justices, ex parte McCarthy* [1924] 1 KB 256 [1923] All ER 233.
25 Ormerod, D, 2008, *Smith & Hogan Criminal Law*, Oxford University Press, Oxford, p7.

2.3 The case of Captain Schröder

It may be useful to summarise the discussion with the case study of Captain Wolfgang Schröder, master of the *Zim Mexico III*, who was convicted of homicide. In March 2006 Captain Schröder had been in command of the vessel, in a compulsory pilotage area, when she collided with a dock-side crane at Mobile, Alabama. The consequence led to the death of a dock-worker, in what mariners worldwide believed to be a mere error of judgement. Captain Schröder was indicted for seaman's manslaughter under 18 U.S. Code § 1115 (Misconduct or neglect of ship officers):

> *Every captain, engineer, pilot, or other person employed on any steamboat or vessel, by whose misconduct, negligence, or inattention to his duties on such vessel the life of any person is destroyed, and every owner, charterer, inspector, or other public officer, through whose fraud, neglect, connivance, misconduct, or violation of law the life of any person is destroyed, shall be fined under this title or imprisoned not more than ten years, or both.*

The jury convicted him and he was remanded in custody for sentence. At his sentencing, Judge Granade noted that the law required jurors to find that Schröder was guilty of simple negligence, a lower standard of unlawfulness more commonly associated with civil disputes:

> *While I certainly do not discount the terrible consequences that have resulted from this negligence, what he has been convicted of is really a civil offense* [sic].[26]

The problem arises in that the characteristics that define guilt in criminal law are very different from those for establishing liability in civil law. That being said, however, the laws of the twentieth century evolved in a process of criminalisation to make a defendant guilty of a crime based upon the principles upon which liability in negligence is founded.

2.4 The accountability of the pilot in command

The safety of air operations reigns supreme among international transport when it comes to statutory regulation; yet, the last long-range airliner that suffered no peacetime fatality was the Handley Page HP 42,[27] which first flew in November 1930.[28] Paradoxically, the most numerous civil airliner

---

26 *United States of America v Wolfgang Schröder* [2007] United States District Court, Alabama Southern District (currently unreported).

27 www.pilotfriend.com/photo_albums/timeline/between/Handley%20Page%20H.P.42.htm.

28 Although all were destroyed during World War II.

today, the Boeing 737,[29] entered service in 1968 and is still in production but, for all the plethora of cutting-edge safety legislation, by November 2014 the 737 family had suffered 341 accidents resulting in 4,293 fatalities.[30] The evidence for the need for statutory regulation to protect safety could not be more compelling.

In precisely the same way as domestic legislation regulates the master's responsibility at sea, so it must regulate the responsibility of the pilot in command. The headline statute is the Civil Aviation Act 1982, which implements the provisions of the Chicago Convention 1944,[31] whose preamble sets out its purpose as,

> *to lay down principles and make arrangements in order that international civil aviation may be developed in a safe and orderly manner and that international air transport services may be established on the basis of equality of opportunity, and may be operated soundly and economically.*

The convention is supported by 19 annexes containing standards and recommended practices (SARPs). The convention runs parallel with UNCLOS in that it provides under Article 1 (Territorial Sovereignty) that '*the contracting States recognize that every State has a complete and exclusive sovereignty over the airspace above its territory*'.

Article 17 addresses the nationality of aircraft in a similar way to that afforded to the ships of flag states and provides that '*aircraft have the nationality of the State in which they are registered*'. Thus aircraft have prima facie the protection of the registered state as if it were sovereign territory and the state is also reciprocally responsible for the international good conduct of its aircraft as regards other states. Airline nationality is not actually addressed in the convention, although it has become an important part of bilateral air agreements, as well as the multilateral transit agreements, which do address ownership in terms of the legal body that exerts substantial ownership and effective control over the aircraft, with the parallel of offshore flags in maritime operations.

Article 44 of the Chicago Convention stipulates that the overall objective of the International Civil Aviation Organisation is to ensure the safe and orderly growth of international civil aviation throughout the world, as such managing the regime envisioned by the convention. The latest revision to Annex 13[32] emphasises the need to develop appropriate legal guidance that will assist states

---

29 By October 2014, 8,263 had been delivered and another 4,037 were on order.

30 www.b737.org.uk/accident_reports.htm.

31 Convention on International Civil Aviation, signed 7 December 1944 by 52 states. As of 2013, the Chicago Convention has 191 state parties.

32 Amendment 11.

to enact national rules to protect information from safety related data collection and processing systems (SDCPS), while allowing for the proper administration of justice in the state; but it cannot dictate to the sovereign regimes of those states how they must define and enforce their own criminal legislative processes, as a result of which international regulation can determine the parameters of a just culture to its heart's content, but cannot influence the administration of justice for the prosecution of offences.

The master's absolute discretion is not so closely paralleled with the authority of the pilot in command, however, which is more narrowly drawn. The 1982 Act gives the authority for the Air Navigation Order 2009, which defines the accountability of the pilot in command for the safe flight of an aircraft: under Part 10, Article 87:

> *The commander. . . must, before take-off, take all reasonable steps so as to be satisfied that it is capable of safely taking off, reaching and maintaining a safe height and making a safe landing at the place of intended destination having regard to:*
>
> (a) *the performance of the flying machine in the conditions to be expected on the intended flight; and*
> (b) *any obstructions at the places of departure and intended destination and on the intended route.*

Article 247 regulates, rather, by prohibition, conduct endangering the safety of the aircraft, in much the same way that section 58 of the Merchant Shipping Act prohibits conduct endangering the safety of life at sea, applying to aircraft registered in the United Kingdom, wherever they may be; and such other aircraft when they are within the United Kingdom or on or in the neighbourhood of an offshore installation:

> (2) *Except where the context otherwise requires, the provisions of this Order in so far as they prohibit, require or regulate (whether by express reference or otherwise) the doing of anything:*
>
> (a) *by persons in, or by any of the crew of, any aircraft registered in the United Kingdom, apply to such persons and crew, wherever they may be;*

A European-wide plan for Standardised European Rules of the Air (SERA), implementing EU Regulation 923/2012, has been delayed in UK jurisdiction, but SERA will replace most, but not all, of the UK Rules of the Air Regulations and there will be a small number of significant changes to UK rules that pilots, air traffic controllers, aerodrome operators and anyone else involved in the operation of aircraft need to be aware of.

SERA.2010 Responsibilities

(a) *Responsibility of the pilot-in-command*
     The pilot-in-command of an aircraft shall, whether manipulating the controls or not, be responsible for the operation of the aircraft in accordance with this Regulation, except that the pilot-in-command may depart from these rules in circumstances that render such departure absolutely necessary in the interests of safety.

(b) *Pre-flight action*
     Before beginning a flight, the pilot-in-command of an aircraft shall become familiar with all available information appropriate to the intended operation. Pre-flight action for flights away from the vicinity of an aerodrome, and for all IFR flights, shall include a careful study of available current weather reports and forecasts, taking into consideration fuel requirements and an alternative course of action if the flight cannot be completed as planned.

Perhaps most critical to the authority of the pilot in command is the provision in the Official Journal of the European Union (13.10.2012) regarding '*Authority of pilot-in-command of an aircraft*':

> The pilot-in-command of an aircraft shall have final authority as to the disposition of the aircraft while in command.

The UN has adopted standards through the International Civil Aviation Organisation; Annex 6, Part II provides:

> 3.2 The pilot-in-command shall be responsible for the safety of all crew members, passengers and cargo on board when doors are closed. The pilot-in-command shall be responsible for the operation and safety of the aeroplane from the moment the aeroplane is ready to move for the purpose of taking off until the moment it finally comes to rest at the end of the flight and the engine(s) used as primary propulsion units are shut down.

As a result, all the signatories must implement these provisions within their domestic law.

United States legislation provides under CFR 14 § 91.3 '*Responsibility and authority of the pilot in command*':

(a) The pilot in command of an aircraft is directly responsible for, and is the final authority as to, the operation of that aircraft.

(b) In an in-flight emergency requiring immediate action, the pilot in command may deviate from any rule of this part to the extent required to meet that emergency.

(c)   Each pilot in command who deviates from a rule under paragraph (b) of this section shall, upon the request of the Administrator, send a written report of that deviation to the Administrator

If there is a parallel with the master's absolute discretion, it is here. The terrible difference between the two, is that in most maritime disasters the master survives to defend the case for which they are held accountable; in most air crashes the pilot dies. But, survive or not, it does not affect the company's exposure to charges of vicarious liability for their acts.

All fatal accidents have a horrifying element, air crashes especially so in terms of what we now call the human element and its consequences. The issues underpinning the criminalisation phenomenon of the key players in civil aviation, therefore, have a direct focus on the determination of what constitutes negligence, and what constitutes gross negligence, and the implications for the prosecution of offenders far beyond pilots and air traffic controllers, as identified by Nemsick.[33] In turn, such issues will have direct consequences upon potential claims for compensatory damages and, in certain jurisdictions, punitive damages. This leads us to the case of the Lexington crash.[34]

2.5 The case of Flight 5191

Comair Flight 5191 was a scheduled United States domestic passenger flight from Blue Grass Airport Lexington, Kentucky, to Atlanta, Georgia, operated on behalf of Delta Connection by Comair,[35] a wholly owned subsidiary of Delta, maintaining its own management and policies, and employing its own pilots.

In the early morning of 27 August 2006, a Bombardier CRJ-100, serial number N431CA, was scheduled to make the flight. Manufactured by well-established aerospace builder Bombardier Commercial Aircraft, the aircraft was a twin-engined regional airliner with capacity for 50 passengers and two crew. On the morning in question it left the stand with 47 passengers and three crew.

---

33 Nemsick, J and S Passeri, 2012, Criminalizing Aviation: Placing Blame Before Safety, accessed via http://apps.americanbar.org/litigation/committees/masstorts/articles/winter2012-criminalizing-aviation-blame-safety.html.

34 See *In Re Air Crash at Lexington*, KY, 501 F Supp 2d 902 (ED KY 2007) (denying plaintiff's motion to remand the case to state court). The court later dismissed punitive damages claims of plaintiffs whose claims were governed by the Montreal Convention. See *In Re Air Crash at Lexington*, KY, 27 August 2006, 2008 WL 1909007 (ED KY 25 April 2008); NTSB: www.ntsb.gov/news/events/Pages/Attempted_Takeoff_from_Wrong_Runway_Comair_Flight_5191_Bombardier_CL-600-2B19_N431CA_Lexington_Kentucky_August_27_2006.aspx; www.ntsb.gov/news/press-releases/Pages/Update_on_NTSB_Investigation_into_the_Crash_of_Comair_Flight_5191.aspx.

35 Comair ceased trading in September 2012.

There was one runway which was operational that morning. Runway 22 (so-called because it was on a heading of 22 degrees) is 7,003 feet long, 150 feet wide and is lighted for night-time use. Runway 26 is 3,500 feet long, 150 feet wide but marked to 75 feet wide, and is not lighted and is restricted to daytime use only. In order to take off from Runway 22, though, it is necessary to taxi across the end of Runway 26. An airport construction project, begun in 2004, was still underway at the time of the accident, necessitating changes to some of the taxiways and signage.

At the time of the accident, there was one air traffic controller in the tower. After handling several aircraft at the beginning of his shift, there were several hours without aircraft movements. In the 20 minutes leading up to the accident, there were three departures under his control, including Comair Flight 5191. The controller on duty at the time of the accident cleared the flight to take off from Runway 22 and to fly runway heading (220 degrees); after providing take-off clearance, he turned away from the window to perform an administrative task and did not witness what happened next.

Analysis of the cockpit voice recorder, the CVR, confirmed that the aircraft was cleared to take off from Runway 22. Instead, after confirming 'Runway two-two', Captain Jeffrey Clay taxied to the holding position, known as the 'short line', for Runway 26, rather than Runway 22, and remained there for about 50 seconds. The aircraft then attempted to take off on Runway 26, which as we have seen was unlit, only a secondary runway, and 3,500 feet long. Based upon an estimated take-off weight of 49,087 pounds, the manufacturer calculated a speed of 138 knots and a distance of 3,744 feet would have been needed for rotation, the point at which the aircraft nose leaves the ground, with more runway needed to achieve lift-off. Clearly the available runway length was insufficient.

The pilot in command handed over controls to First Officer James Polehinke for take-off. The air traffic controller in the control tower was not required to maintain visual contact with the aircraft; after clearing the plane for take-off, he turned to perform administrative duties and did not see the aircraft taxi to the runway.

At a speed approaching 100 knots, Polehinke remarked, 'there is no lights' referring to the lack of lighting on Runway 26. Clay merely answered, 'Yeah', and the flight data recorder gave no indication that either pilot tried to abort the take-off as the aircraft accelerated to 137 knots.

Clay called for rotation but the aircraft sped off the end of the runway before it could lift off. It then struck a raised earth bank, becoming momentarily airborne, before it clipped the airport perimeter fence with its landing gear, and collided with trees, separating the fuselage and cockpit from the tail. The aircraft struck the ground about 1,000 feet from the end of the runway. A resulting fire destroyed the aircraft. Forty-nine of the 50 people on board perished in the accident; most of them were killed instantly in the initial impact. Captain Clay, flight attendant Kelly Heyer, and all 47 passengers were killed; First Officer Polehinke was the sole survivor, with serious injuries including an amputated leg.

During the course of its investigation, the Federal Aviation Administration (FAA) discovered that tower staffing levels at Lexington Blue Grass violated internal policy, which was set out in a 2005 memorandum, requiring two controllers during the overnight shift: one in the tower working clearance, ground, and tower frequencies, and another, either in the tower or remotely at Indianapolis Center, working the terminal radar approach control facilities. At the time of the accident, the single controller in the tower was performing both tower and radar duties. Three days after the accident, the FAA announced that Lexington, as well as other regional airports with similar traffic levels, would be staffed with two controllers in the tower around the clock, effective immediately. No doubt this reflects a sensible response decision but clearly did not invalidate the memorandum retrospectively.

In the casualty report, the National Transportation Safety Board[36] concluded in its findings that the probable cause of this accident was the flight crew's failure to use available cues and aids to identify the aircraft's location on the airport surface during taxi and their failure to cross-check and verify that the airplane was on the correct runway before take-off. Contributing to the accident were the flight crew's non-pertinent conversations during taxi, which resulted in a loss of positional awareness, and the FAA's failure to require that all runway crossings be authorised only by specific air traffic control clearances.

Litigation followed, when civil proceedings were commenced by dependent relatives of deceased passenger Bryan Keith Woodward, who sued Comair, Delta Airlines, the United States government (for alleged FAA errors) and entities associated with Lexington Blue Grass Airport, claiming compensatory damages in negligence and punitive damages in gross negligence. The relevance of the proceedings to this work is that the gross negligence element in the case for punitive damages would expose employers of the blameworthy individuals to the risk of corporate manslaughter.

Relatively early in the case, the plaintiffs applied to the court on a summons for directions for an order that the defendants produce an unedited recording of the airplane's cockpit voice recorder, arguing that the written transcript that had initially been provided was incomplete, that it contained editorial

---

36 Full NTSB sources: www.ntsb.gov/news/events/Pages/Attempted_Takeoff_from_Wrong_Run way_Comair_Flight_5191_Bombardier_CL-600-2B19_N431CA_Lexington_Kentucky_ August_27_2006.aspx; www.ntsb.gov/news/press-releases/Pages/Update_on_NTSB_ Investigation_into_the_Crash_of_Comair_Flight_5191.aspx.

inserts and did not reflect '*the changes in voice tone, tempo, volume and inflection*', which the plaintiffs argued were relevant to the alleged pilot errors, and that the transcripts also did not contain a record of other sounds during the accident sequence that might be relevant to the plaintiffs' pain and suffering claims. Being somewhat concerned about the lack of factual evidence, the court ordered the unedited CVR recovering to be produced to the plaintiffs, observing that '*the recording of the cockpit conversations is one of the few neutral pieces of evidence available to plaintiffs*'.

This case is relevant to another issue, which will be addressed later in this book, concerning the court's ruling on financial penalties. Its relevance goes to the issue of just how the risk was managed, by the key players in the incident, and by the company. Comair had moved to dismiss the plaintiffs' claims for punitive damages, arguing that it was not liable for punitive damages because it did not ratify or authorise conduct of the pilots and that the wrongful actions of the pilots in not conducting a proper pre-taxi briefing, having non-pertinent conversations during taxi (not maintaining a 'sterile' cockpit) and their other mistakes were contrary to Comair's training and procedures. The plaintiffs responded that there was overwhelming evidence that Comair was grossly negligent in its oversight of the airline's safety programme and that the crew's recklessness was foreseeable.

The court found that the plaintiffs '*demonstrated a genuine issue of material fact . . . as to the gross negligence of Comair*', and noted that the plaintiffs had demonstrated notice to Comair of the danger of runway incursions, including a prior incident where Comair pilots took off from the wrong runway, and had proffered expert evidence that Comair practices reflected a reckless disregard for safety.

Of chilling relevance to issues of corporate accountability, the court also found that there was sufficient evidence of the crew's gross negligence to support a finding of punitive damages, including the crew's failure to perform a proper taxi briefing, its violation of a federal regulation and the Comair Operations Manual by engaging in non-essential conversation while taxiing, missing the cues that they were taxiing to the wrong runway, failing to follow proper procedures in determining that the airplane was on the correct runway prior to commencing the take-off, and in failing to abort the take-off even after the first officer recognised that they were on an unlit runway.

During the course of the litigation, the surviving First Officer, James Polehinke and the estates of Jeffrey Clay and Kelly Heyer, with the insurance company of the state of Pennsylvania intervening, filed complaints in the Eastern District of Kentucky alleging, inter alia, that Jeppesen-Sanderson, the navigation chart-makers were negligent in providing incorrect charts to Comair. Jeppesen subsequently filed a motion for summary judgment dismissing the claim against them, which the court granted, concluding that Jeppesen-Sanderson's charts could be utilised to obtain runway information such as length and take-off distances as well as runway configurations and taxiway configurations, and the chart being used by the pilots on the date of the accident showed the prior configuration of the taxiways, not indicating that Taxiway A north of Runway 26 had been closed, but that there was no evidence before the court that the chart had actually misled the pilots, and the plaintiffs' theory of causation was predicated solely on speculation as to potential causes of the crash. Such speculative evidence offers no basis on which a Court can make a finding of fact, which is fundamental to establishing liability in American courts as it is in English courts and the plaintiffs were unable to demonstrate that the Jeppesen chart was a probable cause of the crash. Reluctant to let this particular issue drop, the plaintiffs then filed a motion to reconsider based on newly discovered evidence which they alleged rebutted the court's basis for granting summary judgment. The court denied that motion, finding that the plaintiffs still failed to demonstrate that the Jeppesen chart misled the pilots and was a proximate cause of the crash.

The trials for compensatory damages and punitive damages were severed, with the jury selected first for the trial for compensatory damages. Woodward, 39, was an electrician who lived in Lafayette, Louisiana. Jurors awarded $3 million to his daughter, Mattie-Kay Hebert, who was 15 at the time of the verdict, and $2 million to his other daughter, Lauren Madison Hebert, who was 19 when the panel ruled. US District Judge Karl Forester entered the judgment for the plaintiffs for $7.1 million compensatory damages award. In his judgment Forester upheld the jury award of $1.35 million to his estate for his loss of earning power and $750,000 for his pain and suffering.

The argument for punitive damages followed the plaintiffs' claim that Comair engaged in gross negligence when the pilots used an unlit runway that was too short for a safe take-off, as the National Transportation Safety Board found in 2007, and the United States must share in the blame for gross negligence in that the FAA failed to require that pilots get air traffic control approval before crossing runways, the board said.

The court held:

> *There is no evidence that Comair authorized the pilots to line up and attempt to take off from the wrong runway or that Comair ratified that conduct. To the contrary, the overwhelming evidence is that the Flight 5191 pilots violated Comair training, the procedures in Comair's manuals, sterile cockpit rules, and the required taxi briefing for the first flight of the day.*

In respect of a claim for punitive damages, Judge Forester said Woodward's family had to establish gross negligence by clear and convincing evidence and that Comair *'authorized or ratified or should have anticipated the conduct in question'*.

He said there was no evidence that Captain Clay or First Officer Polehinke, the lone survivor of the crash, had previously committed a similar error or had any history of similar conduct during their year flying for Comair. The judge also rejected the argument that a wrong runway take-off should have been anticipated because of another Comair incident that had taken place in Texas in January 2003. The judge concluded that Comair had very properly incorporated that incident into its safety training programme.

It is also pertinent that the court rejected the plaintiffs' allegations that Comair management exhibited '*a cavalier attitude toward safety*'. The consequence in applying an interpretation to a management failure in such terms to a charge of corporate manslaughter is clear and obvious.

The judge set a trial on punitive damages for 1 February, but on 4 January, postponed the punitive damages trial because of a technical legal conflict over who had authority to make litigation decisions on behalf of one of the plaintiffs. This actually had the effect of giving the parties more time to settle.

In December 2010, Comair had filed a renewed motion for summary judgment, pleading that the claim for punitive damages was misconceived, in part because the case did not meet the requirements of state law. Comair's motion argued that, under state law, a plaintiff must meet two requirements to receive punitive damages from an employer: gross negligence by clear and convincing evidence, and that the employer anticipated the employee's conduct and authorised or ratified the conduct. Comair's lawyers said in the motion that there was no evidence of reckless or wilful indifference and that the airline did not '*authorize, ratify or anticipate*' the conduct of the crew. The motion also noted that during a re-trial review hearing, Judge Forester had observed, '*the question of punitive damages is very iffy, I think*'. The judge said, according to Comair's motion, that there was '*a very real question*' about whether punitive damages should be rendered. The lawyer representing one of the plaintiffs said there was no need to consider the airline's new motion because the law had not changed and that summary judgment motions filed before the trial '*are disruptive and normally not allowed*'. The judge agreed in general terms, but decided to review the issue. In the event, all of the plaintiffs' cases were eventually settled out of court, with the last settlement occurring a day before jury selection for the punitive damages trial.[37]

In respect of air traffic control operations, the NTSB issued the following recommendations to the FAA on 10 April 2007, which accorded exactly with the function of casualty reports, to prevent the recurrence of such accidents in future,

---

37 See *In Re Air Crash at Lexington*, KY, 501 F Supp 2d 902 (ED KY 2007) (denying plaintiff's motion to remand the case to state court). The court later dismissed punitive damages claims of plaintiffs whose claims were governed by the Montreal Convention. See *In Re Air Crash at Lexington*, KY, 27 August 2006, 2008 WL 1909007 (ED KY 25 April 2008).

rather than with any intention to assist with evidence apportioning blame, which will be a relevant issue when we discuss the English case of *Hoyle v Rogers*:

- *Work with the National Air Traffic Controllers Association to reduce the potential for controller fatigue by revising controller work-scheduling policies and practices to provide rest periods that are long enough for controllers to obtain sufficient restorative sleep and by modifying shift rotations to minimize disrupted sleep patterns, accumulation of sleep debt, and decreased cognitive performance.*
- *Develop a fatigue awareness and countermeasures training program for controllers and for personnel who are involved in the scheduling of controllers for operational duty that will address the incidence of fatigue in the controller workforce, causes of fatigue, effects of fatigue on controller performance and safety, and the importance of using personal strategies to minimize fatigue. This training should be provided in a format that promotes retention, and recurrent training should be provided at regular intervals.*
- *Require all air traffic controllers to complete instructor-led initial and recurrent training in resource management skills that will improve controller judgment, vigilance, and safety awareness.*

In addition, the board issued the following recommendation to the National Air Traffic Controllers Association on 10 April 2007:

- *Work with the Federal Aviation Administration to reduce the potential for controller fatigue by revising controller work-scheduling policies and practices to provide rest periods that are long enough for controllers to obtain sufficient restorative sleep and by modifying shift rotations to minimize disrupted sleep patterns, accumulation of sleep debt, and decreased cognitive performance.*

The reader is encouraged to cross-reference this chapter with Chapter 9, when we come to analyse the crisis in civil aviation. The tier of domestic law establishing a framework of responsibility inevitably forms the platform upon which a state's international responsibility must rest, and international legislation in recent years has sought to rationalise this framework in the context of the priority need for flight safety over a priority to criminalise offenders in state courts – but the reality of criminal prosecution, evidence and practice has drifted far from this, with the result that a gulf has emerged between the concept of justice that is understood by the air transport sector and that understood within the normative ethics of society, which is served by the state's judicial regime. Mildred Trögeler rationalised it thus:[38]

---

38 Trögeler, M, 2010, 'Criminalisation of air accidents and the creation of a Just Culture', accessed via http://media.leidenuniv.nl/legacy/mildred-tr-366geler-eala-prize.doc%29.pdf.

One of the main obstacles is that the administration of justice including criminal law constitutes one pillar of state sovereignty and the Contracting States of the Chicago Convention as well as the Member States of the European Union have not exercised the option to delegate this sovereignty function. Criminal jurisdiction remains regulated by national laws. Consequently, harmonisation concerning the balance of these conflicting interests is hard to reach. Instead, the appropriate solution to reconcile these conflicting interests in order to provide for an appropriate administration of justice and enhance aviation safety must be found at the national level.

The core feature of the problem thus remains the fact that, whatever international regulation is attempted, the judicial regime remains jealously guarded as the cornerstone of state sovereignty, which has perpetuated the criminalisation phenomenon through the emergence of criminal negligence, a feature shared between masters, pilots in command, air traffic controllers and beyond. It is this that forms the bedrock of risk that the employer must face in corporate manslaughter.

3   The evolution of corporate accountability

3.1 Manslaughter and the case for gross negligence

This is a central feature of accountability: at the core of the case there must be some blame for gross negligence. An early example is the loss of the *Gossamer*. This early case study in gross negligence manslaughter exonerated the master from blame; and, while the pilot was arraigned, the jury found him not guilty.

On the afternoon of 2 December 1868 the tea clipper *Gossamer* left London bound for Adelaide with a general cargo and was due to pick up passengers at Plymouth. From Australia she would sail on to China and load cargo for the 1869 tea race to London. On board were Captain Thompson (and his wife), the chief mate, Peter Merrifield and the pilot, Andrew Grant. They had been delayed by bad weather but eventually set off and made the Devon coast on 10 December when the wind veered from the north to a southwest gale. It is not totally clear what happened because witness evidence differed but the master had had a conversation with his chief mate about whether or not they would clear Start Point on their current tack and the master thought they would so he told him to stay on the same heading and, then, went below for a sleep having had very little rest over the past two days due to the severe weather conditions. At that point they were nine miles off Start Point, the master having gone below, leaving the chief mate on watch with the pilot. The chief mate told the pilot that he did not think they would clear the land but the pilot thought they would so they held the course, but the chief mate eventually called the master – but it was too late, as there was not sufficient distance for her to tack away from the shore. The master came up on deck and rapidly appraised the situation, casting two anchors, but they broke loose, resulting in the ship drifting back into the rocks just 300 feet from the shore where they launched the boats, which were destroyed in the surf. The coast-guard at Prawle had watched the vessel running into danger and when she was in imminent peril he deployed a rocket launcher to get a line for rescuing passengers and crew to the ship.

Eleven lives were lost but some of these could have possibly been saved. One of the crew, who was a good swimmer, had offered to take the master and his wife ashore but Captain Thompson refused to put himself before the others. When his wife was swept into the sea, he jumped in to save her but both were drowned in the raging surf. Nineteen of the crew and passengers were saved, some by using the line that had been deployed from the shore and others by swimming ashore. Subsequently, the pilot was arraigned on a charge of manslaughter and committed for trial at Exeter. On 7 March 1869 he was found not guilty.

Although it was a criminal case, in order to analyse the professional duty of care we need to understand the underpinning principles of negligence in order to draw a complete picture of the modern law of accountability of corporate manslaughter.

3.2 The foundations of negligence

Street on Torts presents a good starting point for a definition for the law of torts as comprising:

> *the obligations imposed on one member of society to his or her fellows and provides a range of remedies for harms caused by breach of those obligations.*[1]

The main question that underlies the theory of tortious liability is how the law must reconcile the competing interests. An act, even though it is malicious, will not incur such liability unless the interest violated is protected in tort. In the matter of torts, we are addressing the consequence of the unlawful act or omission: has the interest of an innocent third party been violated or not? The mental element is irrelevant: the civil law confines itself to the question as to whether the defendant was to blame for that consequence.

This is precisely identifiable in the evolution of liability for negligence, in which the claimant must persuade the court that it has suffered an actionable and careless infliction of damage as a result of the breach of a duty of care by the defendant. The principles of the tort of negligence were founded upon establishing a duty that arose as a result of the relationship between the parties, and that the duty was broken. In *Grant v Australian Knitting Mills,*[2] Lord Wright emphasised the priority under English law first to establish duty before liability can be addressed; the mere fact that a person suffers loss, even by the act or omission of another, does not by itself give a cause of action against another.

1 Murphy, J, 2012, *Street on Torts*, 13th edn, Oxford University Press, Oxford, p4.
2 *Grant v Australian Knitting Mills* [1931] AC 85 at p103.

The oft-quoted maxim of Brett MR (then Lord Esher) in *Le Lievre v Gould*[3] remains compelling:

> *A man is entitled to be as negligent as he pleases towards the whole world if he owes no duty to them.*

The key to establishing liability, therefore, hinges upon the underpinning evidence that established that relationship in law – evidence that, in civil proceedings, must persuade the court of the claimant's case on the balance of probabilities. Lord Denning famously described the claimant's burden as having to persuade the court on the balance of probabilities that the facts underpinned its case. If, on the underpinning evidence, the court thinks it more probable than not, the burden is discharged; if the probabilities are merely equal, then it has not.[4]

The case of *Donoghue v Stevenson*[5] defines the principles in the current law. In this case the appellant sought to recover damages from the respondent, who was a manufacturer of aerated waters, for injuries she suffered as a result of consuming part of the contents of a bottle of ginger beer, which had been manufactured by the respondent, and which contained the decomposed remains of a snail. The ginger beer had been purchased for the appellant by a friend in a café and arrived at the table in its customary bottle of dark opaque glass, when the appellant had no reason to suspect that it contained anything but pure ginger beer; having had some of the contents poured into a tumbler, which she drank quite uneventfully. Her friend was then proceeding to pour the remainder of the ginger beer into the tumbler when a decomposed snail accompanied the rest of the contents out of the bottle. The appellant claimed damages for alleged shock and severe gastro-enteritis. The appellant further averred that the ginger beer was manufactured by the respondent to be sold as a drink to the public (including the appellant); that it was bottled by the respondent and labelled by him with a label bearing his name; and that the bottles were thereafter sealed with a metal cap by the respondent. She further averred that it was the duty of the respondent to provide a system of working his business that would not allow snails to get into his ginger beer bottles, and that it was also his duty to provide an efficient system of inspection of the bottles before the ginger beer was filled into them, and that he had failed in both these duties and had so caused the event.

---

3 *Le Lievre and Another v Gould* [1893] 1 QB 491. This case underlined the demand for hard evidence of an acknowledged relationship, repeatedly sought in the form of a contract, which underlined the approach of nineteenth century courts; see also *Winterbottom v Wright* (1842) 10 M& W 109; 152 All ER 402; *Heaven v Pender* [1883] 11 QBD 503.

4 *Miller v Minister of Pensions* [1947] 2 All ER 372.

5 *Donoghue (or McAlister) v Stevenson* [1932] All ER Rep 1; [1932] AC 562.

It was Lord Atkin's speech that defined the modern principle, introducing the concept of the *neighbour* as the party to whom the defendant owed a duty of care:

> *You must take reasonable care to avoid acts or omissions which you can reasonably foresee would be likely to injure your neighbour. Who, then, in law is my neighbour? The answer seems to be – persons who are so closely and directly affected by my act that I ought reasonably to have them in contemplation as being so affected when I am directing my mind to the acts or omissions which are called in question.*[6]

Lord Atkin's colleagues illuminated his observation with their own analysis of this redefined principle of duty. It is apparent that *Donoghue v Stevenson* brought evolution, not revolution, to the law of negligence; nevertheless, it was this humble bottle of ginger beer that provided the hard case that led to today's definition of the principles underpinning the tort of negligence, although the principles themselves had not changed. This is well-evidenced by the nineteenth century collision cases in the River Thames, when the underpinning evidence was not contractual but statutory, in the form of the London river by-laws, Admiralty regulations and common law rules on liability – as *Dowell v General Steam* revealed (albeit demonstrating the inconsistency between the bodies of law).[7] That being said, *Donoghue v Stevenson* clarified the principle so that the claimant must establish on the balance of probabilities that:

a) the defendant, the party alleged to be negligent, had a duty to the injured party to avoid acts or omissions that might cause him loss or damage – for example, the master, who is responsible for safety on board their ship, clearly owes a duty of care as a result as regards lawful visitors to the ship, whether or not they are contracting parties;[8]

b) the defendant was in breach of that duty of care, generally by showing that his conduct fell below the reasonably expected standard to be owed by such persons in those circumstances;

---

6 *Donoghue (or McAlister) v Stevenson* [1932] All ER Rep 1; [1932] AC 562, p580.
7 *Dowell v General Steam Navigation Co* (1855) 5 El & Bl 195.
8 Mention must be made of *Caparo Industries plc v Dickman* [1990] 2 AC 605, where the House of Lords held that in novel factual situations, for a duty of care to exist, there must be (a) proximity between the parties, (b) foreseeability of harm/loss and (c) it must be fair, just and reasonable for the law to impose the duty; subsequently applied in *Marc Rich & Co AG and Others v Bishop Rock Marine Co Ltd and Others* [1995] 3 All ER 307; [1995] UKHL 4; [1996] 1 AC 211; [1995] CLC 934; [1995] 2 LLR 299; [1996] ECC 120; [1995] 3 WLR 227; [1995] 2 Lloyd's Rep 299, in which Lord Steyn said that the common law of negligence '*develops incrementally on the basis of a consideration of analogous cases where a duty has been recognised or desired*'.

c)   the claimant must have suffered damage as a reasonably foreseeable consequence of the defendant's breach of duty.

Damages are awarded in compensation with the purpose of putting the claimant
in the position he would have been in, had the negligence not taken place – so
long as that is all that the measure of damages does; they certainly cannot put
the claimant in a better position than he would have been.[9]

   This gallop through the general principles of negligence broadly demonstrates the foundation principle characterising the tort that the defendant's state
of mind – their mens rea, essentially – is not the determining factor in their
culpability. It is this which distinguishes the civil tort of negligence from criminal accountability for manslaughter, as we shall see in Chapter 4. But for now,
we need to make the link which renders the shipowning employer liable for
the wrongs of their employee, the master, which will follow us into criminal
liability.

3.3 Corporate accountability: The issue of vicarious liability

As the era of deep sea maritime trade was truly blooming in the mid-nineteenth
century, it became essential that the investors in the shipping company be persuaded that their money was in safe hands – or at least, as safe as possible under
the circumstances of all the risks that stalked the opportunities for profit. With
no established communication, and few trustworthy agents in far-flung loading ports, the venturers had to place their trust in somebody to protect their
interests, and the master was the most reliable man on the spot. If his ship were
arrested he had to secure her release, and any penalties for port state detentions,
whether legitimate or not, had to be settled and, in many cases, the master had
to raise the necessary funds to pay the fine if need be.[10] He was undoubtedly the
owner's senior manager on the spot, and his absolute discretion would prevail
from the moment he signed the official log book relieving the outgoing master,
until he handed over to his successor.

   The downstream consequence was a logical evolution in the law that charac-
terised the master's special contractual relationship with the owner at common
law, arising out of their common interest in the success of the marine adventure,
which could be relied upon to maintain the bond between them. Slowly, but
with undeniable logic, the master's contractual relationship was developing into
employee, representative, and agent. It was a critical object-lesson in the evolution of the relationship between the master and the owner, which illustrates

---

9 *The Argonaftis* [1989] 2 Ll R 487.
10 HCA 13/78, 24 Oct 1676.

extremely well the principles that define the modern law that renders the owner accountable for the master's criminal negligence.

Employers are vicariously liable for negligent acts or omissions committed by their employees in the course of that employment. On the face of it, the act or omission must either have been expressly authorised by the employer, or the employer must have given instructions that the employee discharged and in the due discharge of those instructions the negligence took place. Of the common circumstances in which a person, such as the shipowner, may be vicariously liable for the torts of its employee, the master, the general rule here is that it is the fact of employment that gives rise to the vicarious liability, not the actions of the employer who may be completely blameless.

The key issue, however, is that liability is not absolute; it is not even strict, but has to be proved on the balance of probabilities. In *Worrow v General Steam Navigation Company*,[11] Alfred Worrow had parked his truck on Butler's Wharf, in London Docks, where he was going to collect some personal property belonging to the second engineer then coming off General Steam's general cargo ship *Starling*. The cases were going to be unloaded by one of the ship's deck cranes, but it was not going to be operated by a hand who was trained in the crane's operation, but by a colleague of the second engineer, Mr Proctor, the third engineer – presumably as a favour. Not only did Mr Proctor not have any training, neither did he have any permission or, indeed, any authority at all to use the crane.

As Mr Worrow was standing steadying a set of crates about to be lowered on to his lorry, he was struck by a case suspended from the jib of the crane. Mr Worrow duly sued for damages. There would not have been much use in suing Mr Proctor, who would probably not have had sufficient assets against which judgment could be enforced and, so, Worrow had to identify whom he could sue. The solution, of course, was to sue the shipowner. He alleged that the defendant company was negligent in that they operated the crane in such a manner as to cause it to strike him; that they failed to keep a proper look-out for persons who were or might be obstructed by or in the way of the case; that they operated the crane in such a way or at such a time as was unsafe by reason of the presence of the plaintiff; and that they failed to warn him that the case or crane was about to be moved or unloaded. Further or in the alternative, the plaintiff alleged that the defendants failed to prevent the crane being operated at the time when the plaintiff was present; that they failed to issue or make any or any proper instructions or regulations concerning the use of the crane at a time when he was in danger of being struck; that they failed to issue or make or to have properly carried out any proper instructions or regulations to ensure that the crane was operated only by persons competent and/or authorised so

11 *Worrow v General Steam Navigation Company Limited* [1950] 84 Ll R 576.

to do; that they failed to exercise any or any proper supervision so as to ensure that the crane was operated only by persons competent and/or authorised so to do or at a time when it was safe so to do, whereby he suffered personal injury, loss and damage.

The company were more laconic in their defence: they denied the main allegations and pleaded that at all material times the crane was being operated by Mr Proctor, with no authority, express or implied, to operate the crane for that purpose or at all. Accordingly, if (as was denied) he was negligent as alleged or at all, such negligence did not occur in circumstances rendering the defendants legally liable. Moreover, they alleged, the accident must have been caused solely, or alternatively contributed to by, Mr Worrow's failure to take sufficient care for himself; after all, he had remained in or near the vicinity of the jib of the crane as the case was being lowered and had failed to look out for his own safety.

The case was heard in the Mayor's and City of London Court, where His Honour Judge Thomas held:

> *Proctor took upon himself to use the crane, and I am satisfied from the evidence that he was not good at it. I think he had some trouble in getting the gears in, and certainly when he swung the case ashore he swung the jib too far and hit the plaintiff with the case. . . . I have to find in this case with regard to Proctor's negligence, which was undoubted, is that he was doing an act which was not in any way authorised or within the scope of his employment – either by implied authority or by practice or in any other way. He was not employed to put ashore the kit of other members of the crew or other officers. . . . And although, as I have said, one sympathises very strongly with the plaintiff, I must in this case find that there must be Judgment for the defendants. . . .*

Far from Mr Proctor going on a mere detour in carrying out his duties, he was negligent while acting on a frolic unrelated to the employer's business, and in this case the employer would not be accountable for vicarious liability. This will be taken further in the case study of the *Tasman Pioneer* which we shall meet later.

The House of Lords' decision in *Lister v Hesley Hall*[12] was not a foundation case in vicarious liability, but it re-states the principle extremely well. In determining whether the employers of a warden at a school boarding house were liable for his sexual abuse of boys in his care, Lord Steyn stated:

> *The question is whether the warden's torts were so closely connected with his employment that it would be fair and just to hold the employers vicariously liable.*

12 *Lister v Hesley Hall Ltd* [2002] 1AC 215.

With relevance to the relationship flowing between the master, or the pilot in command, and their employer, Lord Nicholls brought the case into sharp focus with the point that the close connection between the criminal act of the employee and their contractual obligations to the employer would have to be considered by a value judgement of the court in each case. In the context of the master, the closeness of the relationship can hardly be greater.

To continue the background theme in the evolution of accountability with the China tea clippers, Basil Lubbock had much to say about the master of the clipper ships:[13]

> *No man had more to do with the reputation of a ship than her captain. In the China trade daring, enterprise, and endurance were the* sine qua non *of a successful skipper.... There were many safe, steady goers, but these were not the passage makers. It required dash and steadiness, daring and prudence to make a crack racing skipper, and these are not attributes of character which are often found in conjunction... However there were a few men, who held the necessary qualities of a tea-ship commander, whose endurance equalled their energy, whose daring was tempered by a good judgment, whose business capabilities were on a par with their seamanship, and whose nerves were of cast iron. The clippers, like thoroughbred horses, responded to the master's touch like things of life; Robinson [of the Sir Lancelot], for instance, was said to be worth an extra half-knot on any ship.*
>
> *The strain of a three months' race was tremendous. Some captains only went below to change their clothes or take a bath; others used the settee in the chart room or even a deck-chair as a bed. This was the habit of old Captain Robertson of the Cairngorm, who during the homeward run never turned in but dozed with one eye open in a deck-chair on the poop.*
>
> *Many a man broke down after a few years of it, but the giants, such as Keay [of Ariel] or Robinson, went on and on without a rest, and, still more wonderful, with hardly a serious accident.*[14]

So, in terms of evidence, this provides us with a valuable background in defining the central feature of the master's role: he was primarily the chief risk manager. He still is.

---

13 Lubbock, B, op cit.

14 Lubbock had equally high praise for the crews: '*The crews of the tea clippers would make a modern shipmaster's mouth water. Britishers to a man, they were prime seamen and entered into the racing with all the zest of thorough sportsmen. Many are the stories of their keenness on the homeward run ... In the great race of 1866, the crews of the Serica and Fiery Cross bet a month's pay against each other that they would be first home to London.*' Cope Cornford reflected on the risk of such voyages in the early years: '*These were real seamen, inured to hard fare, wet, cold, want of sleep, incessant toil, imminent danger, and holding a constant loyalty to their employer.*'

3.4 The master–owner relationship

The relationship between the master and the owner, therefore, was founded on the contract of employment between them. A contract is nothing more than an agreement made by the exchange of commercial promises, which is managed by terms that the parties have agreed, or have been imposed by the current law of that jurisdiction and, as a whole, the agreement is recognised by both parties as a legal obligation. The essence of the contract is that it is a bargain – the parties are free to make their own bargain and the terms of the contract must be decided by the parties to the contract.

Whether or not the parties have endorsed a written contract, they will be bound by the terms from the moment when the offer is accepted. From that point, it is all down to how the parties meet the standard of duty that those terms have imposed upon them – ideas that have been moulded by the application of the Golden Rule in normative ethics. If a party fails to perform an obligation agreed in the contract, that must necessarily amount to a breach. The key factor, however is whether the party failed to perform because they had failed to meet the standard of duty promised: that is, the question to be satisfied is, was it their fault? In the non-marine case of *Target Holdings v Redferns*,[15] Lord Browne-Wilkinson held that liability must be based on fault – and it was this that established whether the defendant should be liable for the consequences of that legal wrong in failing to perform the promise that had been made.

The objective of this in the context of the master–owner relationship is to give the parties to a contract of employment the confidence that they can rely on the terms to regulate the way in which it is performed – both by the employer and employee – specifically, to manage the risks that have evolved, with surprising clarity, from nineteenth century maritime trade, in terms of accountability for the way in which the master has discharged his management function on behalf of the owner who appointed him to command of the vessel, not only for the safe navigation of the vessel and the maintenance of order and discipline, but also in relation to the owner's risk.

Given the acceleration and growth of globalisation, which started in the heady days of the nineteenth century Industrial Revolution, it is apparent that the master's relationship with the owner clearly has been moulded by the regulation of this globalisation. Logically, therefore, the normative ethics underpinning this should form the justification for the approach to be taken in understanding the response of societies to the risks encountered in port states and those in flag states. Such approaches necessarily would be subject to the particular hazards faced by the societies in question.

---

15 *Target Holdings Ltd v Redferns* [1996] AC 421.

In fairness, this is the easy part. The hard part will be to characterise the management of the risk of the master's accountability for criminal negligence and for the downstream consequences on the owner. In this context, the changes in the pattern of ship management over the last 30 years have seen the outsourcing of skills, so that the business managing the operation of the ship is often entirely unrelated to the owner. They may well have sub-contracted the crewing contract to another business, who only won the management contract because their tender offered the lowest cost, and any additional financial cost would conflict with the manager's bottom-line budget. Indeed, the manager may be operating with the very minimum of resources, far from able to provide the support that the master might be entitled to expect from the owners of the asset over which they have control. Thus, far from sharing a common interest with the master, the management company today may very well have a vested interest in avoiding legal accountability by dissociating itself from the master's acts or omissions, for it would derive no financial benefit from such association but could be exposed to risk if the master's tortious acts led it into vicarious liability. This is particularly relevant if the master's acts or omissions had given rise to criminal liability, in which a prosecutor may seek to establish that both master and manager shared common features in the mens rea and the actus reus. The management company doubtless would be horrified to face the risk that it might share criminal accountability – such had not been contemplated when it tendered for the work – but, after all, that was why the Merchant Shipping Act 1995 established criminal liability against them for a dangerously unsafe ship under section 98 if they had assumed responsibility for safety in the contract with the registered owner (in that situation the owner would actually avoid criminal liability altogether).

The master in the twenty-first century is expected to be a business manager, something that they had not envisaged in the heady days of their youth as they embarked on their maritime career. Professor Gold touches upon this in his paper[16] in terms of the management of the ship's business; but this does an injustice to the Victorian master who had to do much the same thing. It is just that, in the intervening period, global communications and shifts in the pattern of asset investment had fostered a closer, parental relationship between the master and the owner, which had nurtured the close communication management function in which the master, as the owner's senior manager on the vessel, assumed and discharged responsibility for the company's legal obligations – both civil and criminal. By contrast, Gold illustrates the contemporary situation by

---

16 Gold, Professor E, *The Protection of Masters and Seafarers from Criminalization: Emerging Problems for the Shipping Industry*, Centre for Maritime Law, University of Queensland, Brisbane Prepared for the 31st Annual Conference 'Navigating the Sea of Change' The Maritime Law Association of Australia and New Zealand Adelaide, South Australia 29 September – 1 October 2004.

articulating many of the complaints of today's master, with fatigue high on the list, having to navigate through heavy traffic, sometimes in bad weather, having to make judgments on the safety of the ship in balance with the commercial demands of the shareholders. The consequence of the master's failure under such conditions could lead to a charge of criminal negligence. How the master defends such a charge may well depend on just what decisions the master made as a result of balancing legal duties against commercial demands, and a fatal accident caused as a result of a management failure by the master would trigger accountability for corporate manslaughter today.

The only difference with the master's powers today is that the master has the authority of SOLAS behind him, which is implemented under the UK flag by the Merchant Shipping (Safety of Navigation) (Amendment) Regulations 2011 (SI 2011 No 2978):

> *The owner, the charterer, the company operating the ship (as defined) or any other person shall not prevent or restrict the master of the ship from taking or executing any decision which, in the master's professional judgement, is necessary for safety of life at sea and protection of the marine environment.*

The relationship between the master and owner found its way into statute law, perhaps a little stealthily, following ratification of the Hague Rules 1924, which evolved into the Hague-Visby Rules, adopted by the United Kingdom in the Carriage of Goods By Sea Act 1971. The Hague-Visby Rules provide inter alia that the carrier shall be bound before and at the beginning of the voyage to exercise due diligence to make the ship seaworthy and properly man, equip and supply her.[17] It is the master's personal duty to ensure that the vessel is in all respects safe to proceed to sea, which includes the above requirements – thus, as the master exercises their untrammelled discretion to decide to proceed to sea, they patently make an agency decision that will render the owner accountable to the cargo owner for any damage. The intention of the Hague-Visby Rules was to bring up to date the Brussels Convention 1924, which imposed uniformity into contractual terms relating to the carriage of goods under bills of lading, by striking a balance between the interests of maritime nations and of trading nations. Paradoxically, this afforded the owner the advantage of the nautical fault defence under Article IV, which provides '*that neither the carrier nor the ship shall be responsible for loss or damage to the cargo which was reasonably foreseeable as a consequence of the negligence of the master, or Pilot, or a member of the crew under the master's command*'. In this way, the owner cannot be held accountable for the master's negligence committed while he is on a frolic of his own.

---

17 Art III(1).

Seaworthiness thus is addressed by Hague-Visby for the purpose of regulating civil liability for the loss or damage to cargo but stands as compelling evidence of a vessel's condition, but this will then be applied when interpreting the criminal implications of section 98 Merchant Shipping Act 1995, which renders the master *and the owner* criminally liable if a ship in a UK port, or a UK-registered ship in any other port, is dangerously unsafe. Section 94 defines '*dangerously unsafe*' in the context of being unfit to go to sea without serious danger to human life because of the condition, or the unsuitability of the ship, her machinery or equipment, or if she is undermanned, overloaded or unsafely loaded, or '*any other matter relevant to the safety of the ship*'.[18]

Such a worry does not escape the independent ship manager, for section 98 provides that, if the owner has passed management control over safety matters either directly, by a charterparty or management agreement, or indirectly, under a series of charterparties or management agreements, then the charterer or manager shall simply stand in the owner's place for the purpose of criminal liability under the Act. In all such cases, the master retains responsibility for the safety of life at sea and, indeed, guards still their unfettered discretion as to whether to proceed to sea; in addition to the provisions of the 1995 Act, the risk under current law raises its head if the master's act or omission amounts to criminal negligence. As a result, the master–owner relationship potentially imperils the owner, unless they can mitigate their position by distancing themselves from the master.

It took a maritime disaster to put the law into focus – but it was ever so. In this case, though, it was the law of corporate accountability for manslaughter.

3.5 The turning point for society: The case of the *Herald*

The English Channel is one of the most crowded seaways in the world and, by the time the *Herald of Free Enterprise* and her sisters were bedded down by the mid-1980s, the Dover–Calais run was the most competitive crossing, because it was the shortest – just 22 miles long. The liberalisation of an already cut-throat, competitive marketplace was forcing the boardrooms of ferry operators to consider how best to conduct their prime function: to maximise a yield for their investors.[19] It was against this background that P&O European Ferries had to make some bold business decisions. By the summer of 1986, the boardroom of P&O Ferries was thinking hard about its long-term strategy, in order to keep its position in the marketplace and satisfy the shareholders. This was

---

18 The case of the *Van Gogh* takes us perilously close to human error in the port state's definition of what constitutes a danger to human life, but that is another story. See *Club Cruise Entertainment and Travelling Services Europe BV v The Department for Transport (the Van Gogh)* [2009] 1 Ll R 201.

19 Daniels, S, 2007, *Sea Changes*, Southampton Solent University, Southampton.

the sum of the directors' concerns; safety management was not among their job descriptions. It was surely no coincidence that, at about this time, it resolved to buy out its rival, Townsend Thoresen, reducing the competition and spreading the overheads. In February of the following year, the deal was completed and the directors of P&O Ferries implemented their plans for maximising the financial yield.

Their own ferries on the Dover–Calais route were doing their job very satisfactorily; they did not need Townsend's tonnage there, so it was decided to switch the *Herald of Free Enterprise* to the Zeebrugge route. The only problem was that the linkspans at Zeebrugge had not been designed with the *Herald* in mind, so that, for the vessel's upper vehicle deck to be accessed by the ramp, it was necessary to trim the ship by the head and flood her ballast tanks, to lower the level of the vehicle deck to the linkspan.

When the *Herald* left Zeebrugge on 6 March 1987, not all the water had been pumped out of the bow ballast tanks, causing her to be some three feet down at the bow. Mr Stanley, the assistant bosun, was responsible for closing the bow doors but he had been released from duties by the bosun before the sailing time. He duly went to his cabin and fell asleep; tragically, he slept through the 'harbour stations' call, which ordered the crew to their assigned sailing positions. It was not part of anybody else's duties to ensure that the bow doors were closed before sailing, save the statutory responsibility of the master to ensure that the vessel was in all respects safe to proceed to sea.[20] Her design of clamshell bow doors made it impossible for Captain David Lewry to see from the bridge if the doors were opened or closed, though.

The *Herald* sailed at 19.05 local time, with a crew of 80 and some 459 passengers, 81 cars and 50 commercial vehicles. Passing the outer mole 19 minutes later, she increased speed, when a bow wave began to build up under her prow. At 15 knots, with the bow down three feet lower than normal, water began to break over the main car deck through the open doors at the rate of 200 tons per minute.

In common with other roll on–roll off vessels, the *Herald*'s main vehicle deck lacked transverse bulkheads and, so, the sudden flood of water through the bow doors quickly caused the vessel to become unstable. The *Herald* listed 30 degrees to port almost instantaneously, as water continued to pour in and fill the port wing of the vehicle deck, causing her to capsize 40 seconds later. The *Herald* settled on the sea bed at slightly more than 90 degrees with the starboard half of her hull above water. There had been no chance to launch any of the ship's lifeboats.

---

20 See particularly section 98 of the Merchant Shipping Act 1995 and the applied definitions in section 94.

At least 150 passengers and 38 members of the crew lost their lives when the vessel capsized, the worst disaster for a British vessel in peacetime since the sinking of the White Star Line's *Titanic* in 1912. In accordance with the provisions of the Merchant Shipping Act 1970, a formal investigation was conducted by Mr Justice Sheen,[21] who found fault with the master, chief mate and assistant bosun but, in fairness, the brunt of his condemnation was taken by the management of the owners, finding:

> *All concerned in management, from the members of the Board of Directors down to the junior superintendents, were guilty of fault in that all must be regarded as sharing responsibility for the failure of management. From top to bottom the body corporate was infected with the disease of sloppiness.*

Such findings would logically lead to the question of the owner's accountability. The judge expressed his firm opinion that '*The Board of Directors must accept a heavy responsibility for their lamentable lack of directions*' but, however blameworthy the company was for the failure of management, there was no individual who was part of the controlling mind of the owner culpable for the manslaughter of the souls lost aboard the ship. As a result, a prosecution for corporate manslaughter was misconceived – but, paradoxically, the *Herald* case thus became the midwife of the reform of corporate manslaughter.

3.6 The *Exxon Valdez* experience

The risk of corporate accountability became a very real issue in the boardrooms of shipowners globally, which led to Exxon distancing themselves from Captain Hazelwood and, in the *Exxon Valdez* case, the corporate accountability for the master's alleged negligence was illustrated very clearly indeed. At about nine minutes past midnight on 24 March 1989, the vessel, loaded with about 1,263,000 barrels of crude oil, ran aground on Bligh Reef in Prince William Sound, on the coast of Alaska. There were no personal injuries, but about 258,000 barrels of oil spilled into the sea when eight cargo tanks ruptured. Damage to the vessel was estimated at $25 million and the lost cargo cost about $3.4 million – while the clean-up cost during 1989 was $1.85 billion. It was the worst pollution event in American history at that date, contaminating more than 1,300 miles of coastline, destroying the livelihoods of people dependent upon fishing and subsistence hunting in the region and killing hundreds of thousands of birds and marine mammals; as recently as April 2010 scientists

---

21 *MV Herald of Free Enterprise*, Report of Court No 8074. Formal Investigation (July 1987).

had discovered that residual spill was still being ingested by wildlife and would persist in threatening vulnerable species for decades.[22]

The National Transportation Safety Board's investigation concluded that there were five probable causes of the grounding, only one of which incriminated the owner in that it had failed to supervise the master and provide a rested and sufficient crew for the vessel.[23] But the determination of Exxon's culpability was reflected in the original order of the Federal Court that it pay $5 billion in punitive damages. A federal appeal in 2006 halved it to $2.5 billion and the US Supreme Court further reduced the punitive award to just over $500 million in 2008. More than $2 billion had been spent on clean-up and recovery, while Exxon paid at least $1 billion in damages overall.

There is no doubt that the company, therefore, faced harsh corporate accountability for the spill, while Captain Hazelwood had to accept responsibility as master, when the coastguard suspended his certificate for a period of nine months. He was charged with being drunk at the time of the grounding, although he was acquitted at his trial, but was convicted of a misdemeanour of negligent discharge of oil, for which he was fined $50,000 and sentenced to 1,000 hours of community service. His employer dismissed him.

Unsurprisingly, the owner of a crude tanker would view the *Exxon Valdez* case as a study in the need for caution – and the accountability for the consequence of a risk management failure. In the case of accountability for their master's negligence, though, they had a sound argument to excuse themselves from liability. Mindful of the master's unassailable authority in the safe navigation of the vessel, the owner could argue persuasively that it could not overrule the master in their duty of care and, therefore, the owner should be protected from liability in the event of the master's negligence. This persists as the core feature of the nautical fault defence in the Hague-Visby Rules; what horrifies the shipowning community is the current evolutionary creep of international statutory limitation provisions, by which the (so-far) unratified Rotterdam Rules[24] sweep away the long-established nautical fault defence, with the result that the carrier will be liable for all or part of the loss, damage or delay if the claimant proves that the event set forth is subsequent to a fault of the carrier or their master.

---

22 Esler D et al, 2010, *Cytochrome P4501A biomarker indication of oil exposure in harlequin ducks up to 20 years after the Exxon Valdez oil spill*, Environmental Toxicology and Chemistry, Rice University, Houston.

23 Kolstad, J, 1990, Report Ref M-90–26 through 31, National Transportation Safety Board, Washington DC.

24 Of the 24 signatories to the Rotterdam Rules that were in adopted in 2008, only three to date have ratified: Spain, Togo and the Congo. For its abolition of the nautical fault defence, long may this continue.

3.7 The *Tasman Pioneer*

It was the issue of the nautical fault defence that featured so prominently in the arguments in the case of the *Tasman Pioneer*, and the facts, themselves, provide an extreme case in determining just how a reckless master may or may not incur the vicarious liability of the shipowner. On the evening of 1 May 2001, The *Tasman Pioneer* left Yokohama, bound for Pusan in South Korea, with a passage plan to sail west along Japan's Pacific coast and then via the Japan Inland Sea across the Korea Strait. By the following day, however, the master was concerned that she was running late and, therefore, took the commercial decision to shorten the voyage time by some 40 minutes by taking the channel between the island of Biro Shima and the promontory of Kashiwa Shima, the southwestern extremity of the island of Shikoku. Having altered course he entered the channel at 02.50 on 3 May – but then, disastrously, the ship lost all images on her starboard radar. He apparently realised that he was now in a precarious position and made a command response to abort the passage through the channel. This manoeuvre was not successful, though and the ship struck bottom off Biro Shima with such force that her speed was immediately slowed from 15 knots to some 6 or 7 knots. Shortly afterwards the ship took a list to port and water was discovered in the forward ballast tanks and in the forward cargo holds 1 and 2.

The master ordered the pumps activated but he did not alert the Japanese coastguard, as he should have done, or seek other assistance. The ship then sailed at close to full speed for a further two hours, some 22 nautical miles, before anchoring in a sheltered bay. It was only then that the master contacted the ship managers in Greece, without, however, specifying the cause of damage or its full extent. By the time the salvage team arrived some 14 hours later, the ship was down by the head so severely that the main deck at the forward holds was already under water. Eight days later she was refloated and towed to Onomichi dockyard for repairs. She was declared to be a total loss, however, and was broken up in September 2001.

At the trial[25] Mr Justice Williams took the view that, in this case, the master's initial decision to use the passage east of Biro Shima and his subsequent attempt to abort the transit, were navigational decisions that he had, indeed, taken in good faith – he was endeavouring to save time and keep to schedule, in accordance with his contractual obligations to meet the ship managers' legitimate demands. Where he abandoned his good intentions lay in his actions after the grounding, held the judge; in particular his failure to notify promptly the coastguard and his managers of the casualty and the ship's position and condition; more seriously still, for its implications of dishonesty, in his fabrication of the story that the ship had hit an unidentified submerged object, which could not

---

25 *Tasman Orient Line CV New Zealand v China Clays Ltd and Others* [2010] 1 Ll R 41.

have been motivated by his paramount duty to the safety of the ship, crew and cargo. All those actions, the judge said:

> *can only have been motivated by his implementing a plan designed to absolve himself from responsibility or blame for the grounding and lend a veneer of plausibility to his falsehood.*

In this case, if the bill of lading had fallen under the Rotterdam Rules instead of Hague-Visby, the owners would have been hard-pressed to persevere with the argument that their vicarious liability should not apply to the master's gross misconduct, even though the damage to the deck cargo had occurred as a consequence of the master's efforts to protect his own interests, rather than theirs. With no distinction in English law between negligence and gross negligence, had the casualty resulted in a fatal accident, a potential scenario for corporate manslaughter would have arisen.

Such threats encourage the owner to distance themselves from the master as far as they possibly can, for, if the owner is to be held vicariously liable for such negligence then the consequences in terms of damages may result in punishment that the maritime world had seen first imposed in the *Exxon Valdez* case, involving fines, punishing compensation claims, and plunging share values with which to contend.

3.8 Gathering clouds for reform

The *Herald* case and, in particular, Justice Sheen's comments in the inquiry, sent shockwaves through the industry, and the subsequent failure of the prosecution of P&O for corporate manslaughter did nothing to calm fears that change was being forced in the wake of such disasters. Then, with indecent haste, fate visited the maritime industry again with the *Marchioness* disaster in August 1989. The MAIB report[26] made a number of findings, the principal one being that the collision occurred because neither vessel observed the other until it was too late. Further factors, inter alia, involved design defects that seriously restricted visibility from the wheelhouse of each vessel, both vessels were using the same, middle part of the fairway and the centre arches of the bridges across the river, and clear instructions were not given to the forward look-out of the *Bowbelle*. That being said, the report clearly concluded that there was no wilful misconduct in either vessel contributing to the collision, the foundering or the loss of life, but that some fault lay with those in direct charge of the two vessels at the

---

26 MAIB, 1989, *Report into the collision between the passenger Launch Marchioness and MV Bowbelle.*

time and with those responsible for both the perpetration and the acceptance of their faulty design.

Publication of the report had been delayed in order to accord a fair trial to the master of the *Bowbelle*, Captain Henderson, for failing to ensure a proper look-out and thereby causing damage to another ship and death or personal injury contrary to section 27 of the Merchant Shipping Act 1970;[27] but the first jury failed to reach a verdict, as did the second, and a verdict of not guilty was duly entered on the charge when the Crown Prosecution Service abandoned the case.[28] Subsequently, the MCA conducted a statutory inquiry into Captain Henderson's fitness to continue to hold a certificate of competency, but this took place in 2001, long after the incident, and the MCA properly had to confine itself to considering his current fitness; and the agency had accepted that events that occurred in 1986 have no practical relevance on his current fitness. In his March 2001 report,[29] Lord Justice Clarke did not recommend any disciplinary action against Captain Henderson on the grounds of the length of time that had elapsed and on human rights grounds.

But society's demand for the corporate accountability of the owner for man-slaughter was becoming irresistible.

27 Now section 58 of the Merchant Shipping Act 1995.
28 Butcher L, 2010, House of Commons Standard Note SN/BT/769.
29 Clarke, LJ, 2001, Thames Safety Inquiry: – *Formal Investigation Under the Merchant Shipping Act 1995*, DETR, London.

4 The analysis of reform

4.1 The weakness in the common law

The test of a corporate body's criminal liability for manslaughter had long been dependent upon whether a director or senior manager of the company – part of the 'controlling mind and will' of the company – was personally guilty of manslaughter. This 'identification' doctrine was described in *HL Bolton v Grahams & Sons Ltd*:[1]

> *A company may in many ways be likened to a human body. It has a brain and nerve centre which controls what it does. It also has hands which hold the tools and act in accordance with directions from the centre. Some of the people in the company are mere servants and agents who are nothing more than the hand to do the work and cannot be said to represent the mind and will. Others are directors and managers who represent the directing mind and will of the company, and control what it does. The state of mind of these managers is the state of mind of the company and is treated by the law as such.*

In *Tesco Supermarkets Ltd v Nattrass*,[2] three different judges gave three slightly different interpretations of who could be defined as participating in the controlling mind. Lord Reid stated that the following individuals were controlling minds of a company:

> *the board of directors, the managing director and perhaps other superior officers of a company [who] carry out the functions of management and speak and act as the company.*

Viscount Dilhorne gave a more limited interpretation saying that a controlling mind is a person:

> *Who is in actual control of the operations of a company or of part of them and who is not responsible to another person in the company for the manner in which he discharges his duties in the sense of being under his orders.*

1 *HL Bolton (Engineering) Ltd v TJ Graham and Sons* [1957] 1 QB 159.
2 *Tesco Supermarkets Ltd v Nattrass* [1972] AC 153 (HL).

Lord Diplock stated that the people who form the controlling mind are those:

> *who by the memorandum and articles of association or as a result of action taken by the directors or by the company in general meeting pursuant to the articles are entrusted with the exercise of the powers of the company.*

Mr Justice Taylor had to wrestle with the concept of the controlling mind in the ensuing prosecution of P&O Ferries in the *Herald* case,[3] when he stated:

> *where a corporation, through the controlling mind of one of its agents, does an act which fulfils the pre-requisites for the crime of manslaughter, it is properly indictable for the crime of manslaughter.*

However, although such conclusions highlighted the difficulties of a prosecution against P&O, this did not discourage the Director of Public Prosecutions from pursuing the owners of the *Herald*. Judicial review of the coroner's inquest persuaded the DPP to bring manslaughter charges against P&O European Ferries and seven employees. But it was apparent that the evidence adduced by the prosecution was insufficient to establish the elements of the common law crime of corporate manslaughter beyond reasonable doubt, which demanded that a causal link be established between the company's controlling mind and an individual guilty of manslaughter and, thus, it would be unsafe to direct the jury to reach a verdict on the evidence. As a result there was no case to answer and the judge ruled that the prosecution was not in a position to satisfy the essential 'doctrine of identification'.[4]

4.2 Parliamentary action

Crucially, this also demonstrated the distance that lay between the master and the accountability of their employer in the context of corporate manslaughter; while the Wreck Commissioner held the master responsible[5] for taking the ship to sea in an unsafe condition and whose negligence contributed to the cause of the casualty, without the causal link the company itself was not criminally accountable. Naturally this was consistent with the corporate position with regard to the master's discretion, the foundation for the nautical fault defence in the Hague-Visby Rules,[6] so it all made sense.

---

3   *R v P&O European Ferries (Dover) Ltd* [1991] 93 Cr App R 72.
4   See Richardson, P (Ed), 2009, *Archbold Criminal Pleading, Evidence and Practice*, Thomson Reuters (Legal) Limited, London.
5   *MV Herald of Free Enterprise Report, paragraph* 12.6.
6   Article IV, Rule 2(a).

Meanwhile, the normative ethics of society were pressing its demands for corporate accountability for manslaughter, which became ever more forceful with each successive casualty. Parliament saw P&O's position in the *Herald* case as highlighting an inconsistency with those normative ethics; essentially, society was demanding a corporate head to roll for manslaughter, but the question of fairness made a solution more difficult to divine and this, of course, underpinned the positions adopted by the corporate lobby and the workforce lobby respectively. The attitude adopted by Parliament was particularly noticeable in the wake of the *Marchioness* disaster in August 1989. The MAIB report[7] made a number of findings, the principal one being that the collision occurred because neither vessel observed the other until it was too late. Further factors, inter alia, involved design defects that seriously restricted visibility from the wheelhouse of each vessel, both vessels were using the same, middle part of the fairway and the centre arches of the bridges across the river, and clear instructions were not given to the forward look-out of the *Bowbelle*. That being said, the report clearly concluded:

> *Both vessels were properly certificated, in sound condition, and manned in accordance with the appropriate requirements. In both vessels the bridge or wheelhouse were properly manned. . . . Both vessels were proceeding at a speed which was consistent with the requirements of the Collision regulations and PLA Bye-laws. . . There was no wilful misconduct in either vessel contributing to the collision, the foundering or the loss of life. In as much as personal fault was responsible for the accident, that fault lies with those in direct charge of the two vessels at the time and with those responsible for both the perpetration and the acceptance of their faulty design.*

Before the report was published, the DPP instituted manslaughter proceedings against the master of the *Bowbelle,* Captain Henderson, for failing to ensure a proper look-out and thereby causing damage to another ship and death or personal injury contrary to section 27 Merchant Shipping Act 1970;[8] the first jury failed to reach a verdict, as did the second, and a verdict of not guilty was duly entered on the charge when the prosecution abandoned the case.[9]

It is very apparent that the MAIB found no evidence that might have some probative value towards the culpability of either owner for manslaughter, but this did not discourage Parliament's Home Affairs and Work and Pensions Committees taking partisan and unbalanced evidence arising out of the *Marchioness* disaster, which was published in the First Joint Report of Session 2005–06

---

7 *Report of the Chief Inspector of Marine Accidents into the collision between the passenger launch Marchioness and MV Bowbelle, 1990,* MAIB, Southampton.
8 Now section 58 of the Merchant Shipping Act 1995.
9 Butcher L, 2010, House of Commons Standard Note SN/BT/769.

for the Draft Corporate Manslaughter Bill.[10] Mrs Dallaglio of the *Marchioness* victim support group was invited to give evidence, when she stated inter alia:

> *In every respect of the Marchioness tragedy, from my own experience and what I have experienced within our committee, these companies took Francesca's life unlawfully. . . .*

The chairman commented on the accountability of the owners thus:

> *As the Bill stands at the moment, the companies would be convicted. . .*

The chairman clearly aspired to pursue the function of a court; whether or not as a way to pour oil on the troubled waters of the emotive nature of the evidence that he admitted is open to question but, if that were the case, it failed. When asked whether he thought that there was evidence in the *Marchioness* case that the directors had taken insufficient account of health and safety, witness Mr Perks replied:

> *Indeed, yes. You had people wandering about. . . Can I say it, Chairman? The companies? . . . . Obviously they walked away clapping their hands. We saw them across the road.*

It must be borne in mind that this evidence was being admitted as part of a process to review the current law; the admission of such evidence merely served to devalue its probative value. When pressed for her opinion on whether existing health and safety legislation could be used to identify that somebody had been in breach of that, Mrs Dallaglio replied:

> *I am not a lawyer. I was a woman who was highly traumatised for a lengthy period of time by the loss of my daughter. I put that in the hands of you people here.*

Ivor Glogg, who had been widowed in the accident, had brought a private prosecution which failed, and Mrs Dallaglio was allowed her evidence:

> *He felt very strongly about it. He had his own company. They bankrupted him, these corporate companies. They bankrupted him. He went through God knows how many courts. I attended all of them. Again, bogged down with arcs of visions, technicalities of law, points of law, they were thrown out. . . he was on the verge of going to the crown court then but did not have enough money. They bankrupted him.*

10 HC 540-III.

The emotive nature of the evidence upon which condemnation was brought upon the owner simply flew in the face of the MAIB report, as well as the decision of the stipendiary magistrate in Bow Street Magistrates Court, in the private prosecution brought by Mr Glogg against South Coast Shipping, owners of the *Bowbelle*, and four senior managers of the company, the manslaughter charges being dismissed in June 1992 on the grounds that there was insufficient evidence against any of the defendants to commit them for trial.[11]

This did not discourage Parliament in its mission to satisfy the social demand for corporate criminal accountability, in order to make it easier to get a conviction, whatever the experts might say. That mission was accomplished with the Corporate Manslaughter Act 2007.

In the wider terms of jurisprudence, Parliament's mission may be justified. Society has entrusted to Parliament the function of defining and controlling just what society holds to be a moral wrong; that, itself, is enforced by a power that is maintained quite separately from Parliament and vested in the courts, which Lord Simons described in *Shaw v DPP*[12] as a residual power to conserve not only the safety and order but also the moral welfare of the state.

The normative ethics underpinning concepts of justice bear a heavy burden in regulating criminal accountability. The fairness of criminal justice systems naturally rely on checks and balances and on good faith on the part of legislators and judges[13] to maintain society's moral standards in liability and sentencing. Bauman attaches a very high value to the effect that social and political trends have in moderating the humanity and reasonableness in punitive justice.[14] The emotive responses recorded in the working committee's inquiry in the Corporate Manslaughter Bill naturally informed Parliament's opinion on the contemporary moral standards attaching to corporate accountability; whether the quality of moderation was achieved, remains to be analysed.

The normative ethics of a society naturally characterise its understanding of justice in its own terms which, thus, accords it a subjective definition; but objectively, justice must be envisaged as a set of moral rules that depend heavily on the moderation of society's moral standards. Society evolves in response to internal change and external stimuli and, with it, the concept has evolved of a risk that might threaten the security of that society. Ericson and Carrière have defined this in terms of what they label a 'risk society', in which society has become preoccupied with the concept of risk management for the protection of public

11 Butcher L, 2010, House of Commons Standard Note SN/BT/769.
12 *Shaw v DPP* [1962] 2 All ER 446.
13 Hudson, B, 2003, *Justice in the Risk Society*, Sage, London.
14 Bauman, Z, 1987, *Legislators and Interpreters: On Modernity, Post-Modernity and Intellectuals*, Polity Press, Cambridge.

safety.[15] Naturally the solution that is developed by a democratic risk society delivers a body of legislation that satisfies those crucial normative ethics. But as the history of corporate manslaughter at common law so signally failed to secure convictions against the shipowners, Parliament's solution, to deliver statute law designed to facilitate such convictions, stands in dynamic tension with basic legal rights of fairness, which corporate bodies must share with all other bodies in the eyes of the law. But such a right is exposed to the risk of suspension in favour of the solution that meets the social demand. Hudson's analysis of the risk society can be developed to embrace the rights of all legal bodies, which must confront the risk society's need to trade such rights against the enforcement of the criminal law and consequential punishment:

> *The balance between pursuit of crime control restraints and maintenance of principled limits on punishment is essentially a calculation of what rights, for how long, and with what justification, are to be suspended in the interests of security.*[16]

It is this dynamic tension that led to the iniquity of facilitating convictions through the medium of applying a civil test of negligence: what are the consequences of the defendant's conduct? Rather than the criminal test: what was the defendant's guilty mind?

4.3 Clash of rights

In the maritime context, this can be well illustrated by the case of Captain Wolfgang Schröder,[17] summarised in Chapter 2, leading Judge Granade to comment that, far from deserving criminal accountability, '*what he has been convicted of is really a civil offense*'.

A tort and a crime simply do not share the same properties, either in terms of definition or in terms of their application to the defendant. By contrast with the civil law, crimes are wrongs that threaten the well-being of society to the extent that compensation to the victim is not enough; society must be protected.[18] Save for offences of strict liability, every crime demands the satisfaction of two elements:

1   The actus reus contains all the elements in the definition of the crime except the defendant's mental element. It is generally, but not invariably,

---

15 Ericson, R and K Carrière, 1994, 'The Fragmentation of Criminology', in D Nelken (ed), *The Futures of Criminology*, Sage, London.

16 Hudson, B, 2003, *Justice in the Risk Society*, Sage, London.

17 *United States of America v Wolfgang Schröder* [2007] United States District Court, Alabama Southern District (currently unreported).

18 Allen, C K, 1931, *Legal Duties and other Essays in Jurisprudence*, The Clarendon Press, Oxford.

made up of the defendant's conduct and sometimes the consequences of that conduct, as well as the circumstances in which the conduct took place.

2   The prosecution must also establish the defendant's guilty mind, or mens rea. The primary function of the prosecution case therefore must be to establish the defendant's intention to commit the crime.[19] A result is intended when it is established beyond reasonable doubt as the defendant's purpose – that is, that it was the intended result.

The requirement of mens rea remains the key issue in determining criminal accountability; this most ancient of bastions in criminal law was upheld by Lord Reid in *Sweet v Parsley*,[20] in the presumption that Parliament does not intend to make criminals of people who are not blameworthy for what they did,[21] quoting the venerable Brett J in *R v Prince*:[22]

> *Upon all the cases I think it is proved that there can be no conviction for crime in England in the absence of a criminal mind or mens rea.*

The demands made by the requirement of mens rea on criminal liability require some qualification of the general principle, if a person, who does not intend to cause a harmful result, takes an unjustifiable risk of causing it. Such is the foundation of recklessness, in which either the defendant was aware of its existence or, in the case of an obvious risk, the defendant failed to give any thought to the possibility of its existence.[23]

The constant factor touches upon the defendant's state of mind. In *R v G*[24] Lord Bingham articulated the point beyond any doubt that conviction of a serious crime should depend on proof not simply that the defendant caused (by act or omission) an injurious result to another but that his state of mind when so acting was culpable. Taking an obvious and significant risk by intention or recklessness would satisfy Lord Bingham of a guilty mind but not if the defendant did not perceive the risk. In his words:

> *Such a person may fairly be accused of stupidity or lack of imagination, but neither of those failings should expose him to conviction of serious crime or the risk of punishment.*

---

19 See *R v Moloney* [1985] 1 All ER 1025; *R v Nedrick* [1986] 3 All ER 1.
20 Actus non facit reum nisi mens sit rea.
21 *Sweet v Parsley* [1970] AC 132, at p148.
22 *R v Prince* (1875) LR 2 CCR 154.
23 See *R v Caldwell* [1981] 1 All ER 961; *R v Lawrence* [1981] 1 All ER 974.
24 *R v G* [2004] 1 AC 1034.

4.4 *R v Adomako* and gross negligence manslaughter

A succession of cases over decades exposed the need to define just how evidence of the defendant's state of mind should underpin gross negligence, until, in 1995, the case of *R v Adomako*[25] established that the defendant can be convicted of gross negligence manslaughter in the absence of evidence to his state of mind. In this case the defendant was the anaesthetist during an eye operation on a patient. In the course of the operation the tube from the ventilator supplying oxygen to the patient became disconnected. The defendant failed to notice the disconnection for some six minutes before the patient suffered a cardiac arrest, from which he subsequently died. The defendant was charged with manslaughter. At his trial it was conceded on behalf of the defendant that he had been negligent, in the tortious understanding of the word, and medical evidence was called by the Crown that the defendant had shown a gross dereliction of care. The judge directed the jury that the test to be applied was whether the defendant had been guilty of gross negligence. The defendant was convicted.

Hearing the appeal, the Lord Chancellor, Lord MacKay, referred to the opinion of Lord Hewart CJ in *R v Bateman*[26] in underpinning his conclusion that the criminal law requires a fair and reasonable standard of care and competence in individuals in the position of Mr Adomako, according to the evidence required to establish liability in the civil tort of negligence. This, alone, creates a serious problem in the judicial process, for, in civil cases, the claimant must persuade the court that it has proved on the balance of probabilities the requisites for establishing liability, whereas in criminal cases, the prosecution must persuade the court that the case against the defendant is proved beyond reasonable doubt, by applying the evidence to the body of criminal law with all those characteristics special to it, that is, including the mens rea.

As if the mischief in the court's decision were not clear enough, however, the judge further held that:

> *in order to support an indictment for manslaughter the prosecution must prove the matters necessary to establish civil liability (except pecuniary loss), and, in addition, must satisfy the jury that the negligence or incompetence of the Accused went beyond a mere matter of compensation and showed such disregard for the life and safety of others as to amount to a crime against the State and conduct deserving punishment.*

The judge's observations on the application of civil liability massively outweigh that devoted to criminal liability; but, to summarise the principle in this case, the jury needs to consider whether:

---

25 *R v Adomako* [1995] 1 AC 171.
26 *R v Bateman* (1925) 19 Cr App R 8 (at pp12–13).

- the defendant owed a duty of care to the deceased; and
- he was in breach of that duty; and
- the breach was so grossly negligent that it should be seen as criminal; in Lord MacKay's words:

> . . . *gross negligence . . . depends . . . on the seriousness of the breach of the duty committed by the defendant in all the circumstances in which he was placed when it occurred and whether, having regard to the risk of death involved, the conduct of the defendant was so bad in all the circumstances as to amount in the jury's judgment to a criminal act or omission.*

The whole issue of the defendant's state of mind, his mens rea for the crime, has therefore been put into the form of an objective test determined by the circumstances and grafted on to the evidential test required for liability in civil proceedings. At least, that is, for manslaughter; the requirements to establish guilt for criminal damage bring us back to the logic of the House of Lords decision in *R v G*, which demanded that the subjective standard should apply; but in the case of corporate manslaughter you need an individual to whom the standard must be applied, and that would not suit Parliament's needs at all.

Ultimately, the yawning gap between civil and criminal liability was, and remains, the burden of proving the essential elements; if put to the test in criminal proceedings, the jury must consider some ethereal concept that criminalises what is essentially a tortfeasor, but in this case is the criminal defendant, and the only way in which the law has developed that, as seen in *Adomako*, obliges the jury to apply an objective standard to a test for establishing a guilty mind. At the very least, the concept of criminal negligence is vague and open to interpretation, that is, its very definition is subjective. To establish such culpability by an objective test invites its rejection.

Speaking in the London Shipping Law Centre's 8th Cadwallader Memorial Lecture in 2005, Epaminondas Embiricos took the part of advocate for the industry, making a valid point in a critical analysis of the EU Directive on Criminal Sanctions for Ship Source Pollution:

> *The term 'serious negligence' is vague, subjective and ill defined. Yet, it is a fundamental principle that criminal law must be clear and specific. Thus, the term 'serious negligence' is legally defective and inconsistent with the global regime. It is imprecise, subjective and lacks clarity and will therefore be most prejudicial to the accused in the climate of public sentiment commonly experienced after a pollution incident.*[27]

---

27 See Transcript of the 8th Cadwallader Annual Memorial Lecture: The Extra-Territorial Jurisdiction in Criminalisation Cases: Sovereign Rights in Legislation and New Risks for the Shipping Industry, 2005, The London Shipping Law Centre, UCL, London.

If behaviour is to be the subject of control by criminal law, it is essential that the law in question is, at the very least, precise. The courts must apply the definition of the crime according to the intention of the body that legislated it and, so, they are presented with an exceptional problem when the intention of Parliament is impossible to fathom in a given circumstance, such as with a term that is vague and whose defining principles were founded on decisions in civil proceedings whose process is different from that in question – as we find in the situation in which the modern law of negligence, stemming from a claim for damages arising out of a bottle of contaminated ginger beer[28] that must be determined on the balance of probabilities according to civil evidence procedures, has driven the criminal law in which criminal evidence procedures must deliver a verdict beyond reasonable doubt.

The master's accountability necessarily hinges upon their judgment, in which they have the discretion allowed in current law, as it has allowed for generations, to make decisions about what to do and when to do it. How they discharge the burden of their accountability will be determined by their awareness, or conscious assumption, of the risk that will follow. If they hold their belief in the consequences genuinely, then they will have discharged their burden in criminal law – with the aside of Lord Bingham's wisdom that, the more unreasonable the belief, the less likely it is to be accepted as genuine.

The ultimate point is that, if the master were not held to be guilty of gross negligence manslaughter, then there would not have been a conviction upon which the controlling mind of their employer would be accountable for corporate manslaughter. The crux of any reform, therefore, had to address this as the defining issue in a Bill that was intended to make it easier to satisfy society's ethical demand to punish the shipowner.

In the light of the Law Commission's report in 2000[29] the Select Committee on Home Affairs and Work and Pensions set its face to drafting a Bill that reflected the Government's determination to enable more prosecutions to proceed by tackling the difficulties created by the identification principle.[30] The new proposals were intended to change the basis of liability from the requirement of identifying the causal link from an individual guilty of manslaughter to the controlling mind of the company, to liability founded on accountability for the way in which an organisation's activities are managed or organised by its senior managers.[31] In this way it was the intention

---

28 *Donoghue (or McAlister) v Stevenson* [1932] All ER Rep 1; [1932] AC 562.
29 *Reforming the Law on Involuntary Manslaughter: The Government's Proposals* (Home Office, May, 2000, CC NO77828).
30 Home Affairs and Work and Pensions – First Report, Session 2005–06, December 2005.
31 Home Office, Corporate Manslaughter: The Government's Draft Bill for Reform, Cm 6497, March 2005.

of Parliament to close down the possibility that a shipowner could avoid criminal liability for corporate manslaughter, in the way encountered in the case of the *Herald*.

The Corporate Manslaughter and Corporate Homicide Act 2007 was the result.

5 What society wanted, and what society got

The Corporate Manslaughter and Corporate Homicide Act 2007

5.1 Overview

The crime of corporate manslaughter is, broadly, committed when an organisation owes a duty to take reasonable care for a person's safety and the way in which activities of the organisation have been managed or organised amounts to a gross breach of that duty and causes the person's death. How the activities were managed or organised by senior management must be a substantial element of the gross breach. The mischief of criminal negligence stalks through the statute, stating, as it does, that the defendant organisation owes a relevant duty of care to the victim according to the common law of negligence – clearly giving its support to the old ill as the common law of negligence, which is simply and conveniently nipped and tucked to fit a criminal process that must respond to the baying crowds for some criminal accountability that meets their normative ethics, notwithstanding any irritating issues of jurisprudence that may get in the way.[1]

For the shipowner, the serious issue is that there need no longer be a causal link between the fatality and the controlling mind of the company; now the master's behaviour may incriminate them because the death must have been caused merely by a management failure; it need not even have been the sole cause of death, but if the master, who, after all, plays significant strategic or regulatory compliance roles in the management of the whole or a substantial part of the organisation's activities, behaves in such a way that their conduct falls far below what could reasonably have been expected, then the shipowner will be guilty of the offence.[2]

As if to remove any lingering doubt or loophole in the application of the 2007 Act, section 28 specifically applies the offence to any ship or aircraft that

---

1 Anon, 2007, *Corporate Manslaughter and Corporate Homicide Act 2007 – Explanatory Notes*, HMSO, London.
2 See Anon, 2010, *Corporate Manslaughter & Health and Safety Offences Causing Death – Definitive Guideline*, Sentencing Guidelines Council, London.

is within the UK's sovereign jurisdiction of the territorial sea or airspace at the time when the harm occurs that ultimately results in death, and to any UK-registered ship anywhere in the world, whether or not any mishap occurred that led to the foundering of the ship or aircraft. Overall, the drafting experts made a thorough job of ensuring that the Act would be applied vigorously to the maritime or aviation scenario; and there is no doubt that companies are understandably shy of exposing themselves any more than is absolutely essential to such a risk. The master's conduct is not necessarily fatal to the company's position – but the potential for criminal litigation is obvious. For example, there is no doubt that Tasman Orient Line had excellent company standing orders in place in the case of the *Tasman Pioneer*,[3] demonstrating a management system that would successfully pass any test of reasonableness; what would be open to issue, was how the master's conduct in that case may have incriminated the company.

For all that, the master–owner relationship presents a strong contractual bargain that is founded on a particular function, in which the master, or the pilot in command, has a risk management function to perform. To this extent, the contract contains rights and obligations that benefit both parties across the entire range of the activities that the company would wish to protect. The resultant picture shows a pattern of advantages to the relationship that far out-weigh the risk to the company. And, after all, the spectre of vicarious liability has evolved as a sword that can be wielded against and by the employer. The historic case of *Lister v Romford Ice*[4] underlines the general rule that the mere fact of employment will give rise to vicarious liability but, under the terms of their contract, the employee must be diligent and use reasonable skills while at work. This amounts to a general duty to take reasonable care while at work, which is owed to the employer, as opposed to any tortious liability to a third party who suffers loss as a result of the employee's negligence. As a consequence, the master may be sued by the shipowner for breach of the employment contract if the former's negligence leads to loss by the latter, whether in terms of civil damages or of a fine. While the shipowner would be insured against the quantum of damages, it could not insure itself against the criminal penalty of a fine; but as a claim in civil compensation against the master, it may certainly be recoverable. That, of course, is a matter of com-mercial bargain with which the state could not interfere.

But it is the contract between them that establishes the trigger of a manage-ment failure, upon which the 2007 Act depends.

---

3   *Tasman Orient Line CV v New Zealand China Clays Ltd and Others* [2010] 2 Ll R 13.
4   *Lister v Romford Ice and Cold Storage Co Ltd* [1956] AC 555.

5.2 The Act in summary

The offence is described in section 1, by which an organisation is guilty of an offence if the way in which its activities are managed or organised (a) causes a person's death, and (b) amounts to a gross breach of a relevant duty of care owed by the organisation to the deceased. But it is guilty of an offence only if the way in which its activities are managed or organised by its senior management is a substantial element in that breach. For the purposes of this Act, a '*relevant duty of care*' for the shipowner means any of the following duties owed by it '*under the law of negligence*', namely a duty owed to its employees or to other persons working for the organisation or performing services for it; a duty owed as occupier of premises; a duty owed in connection with the supply of goods or services, the carrying on by the organisation of any construction or maintenance operations, the carrying on by the organisation of any other activity on a commercial basis, or the use or keeping by the organisation of any plant, vehicle or other thing. As if that were not enough, it can be understood that duties of care commonly owed by shipowners include the duty owed by an employer to his employees to provide a safe system of work, whether that be shipboard or shoreside, and will include dock workers or others working on the ship. Naturally, duties of care also arise out of the activities that are conducted by shipowners transporting passengers and lawful – as well as unlawful – visitors.

A breach of a duty of care by an organisation is a 'gross' breach if the conduct alleged to amount to a breach of that duty falls far below what can reasonably be expected of the organisation in the circumstances; '*senior management*' means the persons who play significant roles in the making of decisions about how the whole or a substantial part of its activities are to be managed or organised, or the actual managing or organising of the whole or a substantial part of those activities.

The explanatory notes state that this reflects the position under the common law offence of gross negligence manslaughter and, by defining the necessary relationship between the defendant organisation and victim, sets out the broad scope of the offence. Thus, while the common law offence of manslaughter by gross negligence is abolished in its application to corporations, the key mischief of applying the principles of civil liability modified for criminal accountability remains.

Section 8 addresses factors for the jury to consider if it is established that an organisation owed a relevant duty of care to a person, and it falls to the jury to decide whether there were a gross breach of that duty. The jury must consider, for example, whether the evidence shows that the organisation failed to comply with any health and safety legislation that relates to the alleged breach and, if so, how serious that failure was and how much of a risk of death it posed. Of course, the complexity arises, in this respect, in that 'failure to comply' must be isolated from 'liability', for the strict liability required in health and safety offences turns the burden of proof on to the defendant to prove due diligence, an alien concept in the establishment of negligence at common law, which is demanded by section 2(1). As a result, statutory duties owed under health and safety law are not relevant duties for the purpose of the 2007 Act.[5]

Subsection 3 allows the jury also to consider the extent to which the evidence shows that there were attitudes, policies, systems or accepted practices within the organisation that were likely to have encouraged any such failure as is mentioned in subsection (2), or to have produced tolerance of it; and to have regard to any health and safety guidance that relates to the alleged breach. The need for expert evidence to enlighten the jury's understanding must be applied to the eye-witness evidence, particularly in the case of a large shipowning company with complex management structures; at least such a prosecution will provide gainful employment to maritime consultants, whose opinions must, yet, be explained with clarity to jurors whose knowledge of shipboard management is unlikely to embrace rapid comprehension. But then subsection (4) states that the jury may still consider any other matters they feel to be relevant – and in a case in which emotive issues are admitted in evidence, such vague guidance presses hard on the concept of fairness, indeed, on the chance of an appeal against conviction if the judge misdirected it.

In order to keep the matter in sharp focus, the Sentencing Guidelines Council emphasised the obligation on the prosecution to prove each of these elements to the criminal standard required of this Act, as well as pointing out the contrast between corporate manslaughter and strict liability offences enacted under health and safety laws, which require the establishment of a due diligence defence if liability is to be avoided.[6]

The glaring issue, then, compels the prosecution in a corporate manslaughter case to establish beyond reasonable doubt that the breach of duty of care was a significant cause of death, although it need not be the only cause, while the more modest demands upon an indictment containing health and safety counts allow the prosecution to establish guilt against a company without having to adduce evidence that injury was caused by the failure to ensure safety; it would then be for the company to establish a due diligence defence. The issue turns on the requirement under corporate manslaughter to establish both a gross breach of duty of care and some senior management failure as a substantial element in that breach, the effect of which demands that the prosecution will generally need

---

5 See Ministry of Justice, 2007, *A Guide to the Corporate Manslaughter and Corporate Homicide Act 2007*, HM Government, London.

6 Sentencing Guidelines Council, 2010, *Corporate Manslaughter & Health and Safety Offences Causing Death – Definitive Guideline*, SGC, London.

to establish a failure in the management system; by contrast the strict liability raised in health and safety offences demands that the successful defendant must show that it was not reasonably practicable with due diligence to avoid a risk of injury or lack of safety. If, in this circumstance, the management failure is at an operational rather than systemic level, then, for example, the master's negligence may only lead to a minimal failure to reach the standard of reasonable practicability demanded by the Act. In this case the company will not be held accountable for manslaughter.

For the bewildered shipowner, the serious issue underlying the new statute can be epitomised in the fact that there need no longer be a causal link between the fatality and the controlling mind of the company; now the master's behaviour may incriminate their employer even though they are not part of the controlling mind of the company, because the death must have been caused merely by a management failure; it need not even have been the sole cause of death, but if the master, who, after all, plays significant strategic or regulatory compliance roles in the management of the whole or a substantial part of the organisation's activities, behaves in such a way that their conduct falls far below what could reasonably have been expected, then the shipowner will be guilty of the offence.[7] It must be said, that this introduces an inconsistency with the legal theory that underlays corporate responsibility for the master's unassailable discretion, which is currently enshrined in SOLAS Chapter V Reg 34 and duly amended very slightly in English law by 2011 Regulations.[8,9] If the shipowner is now to be responsible criminally for the exercise of the master's discretion, then it must logically demand that the shipowner must have the power to override the master in the exercise of that discretion, which of course offends SOLAS as well as the provisions of Code 5 of ISM.[10]

5.3 The Act at work

There is no doubt that Parliament, trade unions and many commentators hailed the dawn of the 2007 Act as the new era in criminal justice, finally sweeping away the flawed common law system that they saw as protecting corporate offenders from accountability for manslaughter. For them, it could not come a moment too soon, following the dismal failure of the prosecution to deliver

---

7 Ibid.

8 The Merchant Shipping (Safety of Navigation) (Amendment) Regulations 2011 (SI 2011 No 2978), in force from February 2012.

9 Of course, while the master's discretion is unassailable, their personal accountability is not.

10 International Safety Management Code 2002, 5.2: The company should establish in the safety management system that the master has the overriding authority and the responsibility to make decisions with respect to safety and pollution prevention and to request the company's assistance as may be necessary.

convictions for corporate manslaughter in the Hatfield train crash case. On 17 October 2000, a GNER passenger train from London to Leeds had crashed following the catastrophic failure of a worn and broken rail outside Hatfield station, which had been previously identified as requiring replacement, but for a catalogue of reasons had not been repaired. After final hearings in 2005, it was apparent that prosecutions against Balfour Beatty and Network Rail had failed under the old common law offence. The corporate defendants had pleaded guilty to statutory health and safety breaches, but such strict liability offences did not meet the demands of the normative ethics of society for criminal account-ability. As a result, there was a great deal of pressure on the Crown Prosecution Service to demonstrate the success of the new Corporate Manslaughter Act. Perhaps it would have been all the more impressive had the first successful pros-ecution been against a large corporate employer whose culpability and means would create a publicity success for the new Act. As it was, the defendant was a small technical consultancy.

5.4 The case against Cotswold Geotechnical Holdings Limited[11]

The case arose out of the death of a geologist who was killed in 2008 when a trial pit in which he was working collapsed on top of him. Alexander Wright was employed by Cotswold Geotech as a junior geologist, when he was taking soil samples from inside a pit that had been excavated as part of a site survey, when the sides of the pit collapsed, crushing him. In addition to the charge under the 2007 Act, the company was charged with failing to discharge a duty contrary to section 33 of the Health and Safety at Work etc. Act 1974.

The prosecution case was that Cotswold Geotech had failed to update and comply with its own risk assessments, and had failed to take all reasonably prac-ticable steps to prevent the deceased from working in a dangerous way.

By virtue of section 1 of the 2007 Act, the company prima facie would be guilty if the way in which its activities were managed or organised (a) caused Mr Wright's death and (b) amounted to a gross breach of a relevant duty of care owed by the company to the deceased. Section 1(3) required that, once this had been established, the prosecution had to prove that the way in which the company's activities were managed or organised by its senior management was a substantial element in the breach of the relevant duty of care.

The jury returned a verdict of guilty.

Taking the step beyond the question of liability, sentencing was addressed, in the guidelines published by the Sentencing Guidelines Council in 2010,

---

11   *R v Cotswold Geotechnical (Holdings) Ltd* [2011] ALL ER (D) 100 (May).

which ominously counselled the sentencing judge to look carefully at both turnover and profit, and also at assets, in order to gauge the resources of the defendant. Cotswold Geotech arguably escaped lightly with a fine of just £385,000 which was to be paid over ten years at a rate of £38,500 per annum. It was certainly less than the starting point of £500,000 recommended by the Sentencing Guidelines Council – and the plea in mitigation of a shipowner with significant assets and cash reserves might not be received so sympathetically. Not that Cotswold Geotech found it particularly sympathetic, but Mr Justice Field concluded:

> *It may well be that the fine in the terms of its payment will put this company into liquidation. If that is the case it's unfortunate but unavoidable. But it's a consequence of the serious breach.*

Individuals cannot be prosecuted under the Act and Peter Eaton, the company's sole director, was charged separately with the common law offence of gross negligence manslaughter.[12] But there was the rub, as well, for this was clearly a small company, the sort of entity (and the only sort of entity) that had previously been successfully prosecuted under the common law, in which it was easier for the prosecution to incriminate senior management and their role within the company. A larger company has yet to face prosecution; as a result, the conviction in this case sheds very little light on just how more effective the 2007 Act will be in securing convictions than the old common law requirement for an individual to be convicted, whose causal link with the company's controlling mind can be established. It was, in effect, just as simple as the case of *R v OLL and Kite.*[13]

In November 1994, OLL Limited, an outdoor activity company, and its managing director Peter Kite, were convicted of the manslaughter of four students of Southway Comprehensive School in Plymouth, aged between 16 and 17, who died during a canoeing trip in Lyme Regis, Dorset in March 1993. OLL had organised and managed the basic canoe course; but the two instructors whom OLL had sent out to sea with the students on the course were little wiser than the students, for their expertise had been limited to a three-day training assessment, just one week earlier, in which they had received the basic canoe instructions that they were expected to pass on to the teenagers. They had both been placed in the novice group and were barely competent to undertake the journey themselves, let alone be put in charge of the students. Nine months earlier, two experienced instructors had written to the centre about levels of safety and warned that unless standards of safety were improved, '*you may find*

---

12 He was also charged with an offence under the Health and Safety at Work etc Act 1974 but, in the event, the court held that he was too ill to stand trial.

13 *R v Kite and OLL Ltd* (the 'Lyme Bay' case), Winchester Crown Court, 8 December 1994, unreported.

yourselves trying to explain why someone's son or daughter will not be coming home'. They resigned; Mr Kite carried on regardless.

Horrifyingly, but more horrifying because of the prediction of the two former instructors, the group was swept out to sea, and capsized frequently. The centre had not provided any distress flares and had not informed the coastguard of the expedition. OLL was convicted of corporate manslaughter under the prevailing common law and was fined £60,000. Mr Kite was sentenced to three years' imprisonment (reduced to two on appeal); the centre's manager Joseph Stoddart was acquitted of manslaughter.

The key issue in this study is that size matters. OLL was a small company and proving that Mr Kite was its 'controlling mind' and had acted negligently was easily achieved. Cotswold Geotech was an equally small company and the prosecution would have been able to establish that Mr Eaton had been its 'controlling mind' just as easily as it had been able to prove a 'management failure' resulting in Mr Wright's death. Writing in the *Law Society's Gazette* on the 3 March 2011, David McCluskey expressed the sage opinion that the test of the new law has not yet come, and will not come until a large company with a large board of directors, faces prosecution.[14]

But such a prosecution is a long time coming. Lion Steel Equipment Ltd is a large company, with capital of some £1.5 million,[15] and has been indicted following the death of an employee who fell through the roof of an industrial unit at the company's Hyde headquarters in 2008. The company has also been charged under sections 2 and 33 of the Health and Safety at Work etc. Act 1974 (HSWA) for failing to ensure the safety at work of its employees.

In addition, three of the company's directors have each been charged with gross negligence manslaughter and also face charges under section 37 of HSWA for failing to ensure the safety at work of their employees.

So far, therefore, analysis of the effect of the new Act upon shipowners could be little more than speculation. But it may be worthwhile to speculate, with a case study based on a recent casualty. Mature and reflective analysis must await the publication of an accident report before rushing to judgment in the case of the *Costa Concordia*, which resulted in the deaths of 28 people. When the death toll had reached only six, and before the primary sources of evidence had been analysed, Costa's chief executive Pier Luigi Foschi, categorically put the blame on the master, emphasising the master's absolute discretion in matters of navigation (presumably under SOLAS V), although confirming that deviations from the passage plan would be made with company approval during bad weather or if a vessel faced other navigational dangers.[16] Somewhat damningly, Mr Foschi

14 McCluskey, D, 2011, *The Law Society's Gazette*, The Law Society, London.
15 Annual Return of Company Information (ARO1) 15 February 2012.
16 Eason, C, *Lloyd's List*, 16 January 2012, Informa plc, London.

described as rash the master's decision to '*showboat the ship*' within 500 metres of the island of Giglio.

In February 2012, Nautilus International cautioned against such rush to judgment[17] and General Secretary Mark Dickinson emphasised, rather, the importance of addressing safe manning and associated issues of hours of work, competence of crew and training issues, all of which are fundamental points addressed by the STCW Convention.[18] Notwithstanding the corporate manslaughter legislation adopted by Italy in 2008, we need to confine ourselves to the relevance of an intriguing question: what if the *Costa Concordia* had foundered in UK territorial waters?

By virtue of section 1 of the 2007 Act, the owner of the vessel would be accountable for corporate manslaughter if the way in which its activities were managed or organised by its senior management – be it a senior director or the master of the vessel whose responsibility was highlighted by Mr Foschi – caused, or contributed a substantial part in the deaths of the innocent people, and amounted to a gross breach of a relevant duty of care owed by the organisation to the deceased. The relevant duty of care would be that owed by the company under the law of negligence. If the master, with the absolute discretion at his disposal, had indeed pursued a 'frolic of his own', contrary to the company's shipboard management system, then would it be fair that this company, with its massive size and highly complex management structure, should be held accountable for the deaths of the 28 people on board? Whatever the answer, in order to discharge its function under section 8, the jury would have to consider, firstly, whether there had been a management failure and, if so, whether the conduct that constituted this failure fell far below what could reasonably have been expected of that management. The evidence that they will consider, however, may be wider than one might expect if its probative value allows them to consider the extent to which there were attitudes, policies, systems or accepted practices within the organisation that were likely to have encouraged any such failure, or to have produced tolerance of it, particularly if convention issues from SOLAS to STCW are held to be relevant.

For the lawyer who must advise shipowners on their corporate accountability under the new 2007 Act, such speculation will, of course, have to wait upon further decisions such as that in Lion Steel, which inevitably will precede the conclusions on evidence in the *Costa Concordia* casualty. And speculation is always a dangerous thing: but it is intriguing, nevertheless.

---

17 Anon, *Telegraph*, February 2012, Nautilus International, London.
18 International Convention on Standards of Training, Certification and Watch Keeping for Seafarers, 1978, with special reference to the Manila Amendments 2010.

5.5   The case against Lion Steel Equipment Limited[19]

Lion Steel Equipment Limited manufactures and distributes storage equipment from two factories, at whose Hyde, Manchester premises it employed Steven Berry. In 2008, he fell through a rooflight to his death. Ever since the Crown had failed to secure a conviction against P&O Ferries for the *Herald of Free Enterprise* disaster,[20] the normative ethics of society had been demanding new legislation that would sweep away the frailties in the common law and punish companies for criminal mismanagement that had led to fatal accidents. There had been a successful prosecution in England and Wales under the Corporate Manslaughter and Corporate Homicide Act 2007 in the case against Cotswold Geotech Holdings[21] but, in fairness, this company had been so small that the old common law offence, demanding, as it did, a causal link between the criminal act and the controlling mind, would probably have been just as effective.[22] Lion Steel was described by the trial judge as being 'not a large firm'; with a turn-over exceeding £10 million per annum and a workforce of 142 employees, the anticipation, however, lay in the fact that here, at last, was a company that was large enough to test the capability of the 2007 Act in corporate accountability, and succeed where the common law had failed. In terms of the evolution of the law, the prosecution against them under the new Act promised to demonstrate the value of this new generation of corporate accountability, which would succeed where the old common law had failed.

It will be recalled that section 1 of the 2007 Act renders the company guilty if the way in which its activities were managed or organised (a) caused the victim's death and (b) amounted to a gross breach of a relevant duty of care owed by the company to the deceased. The demands of section 1(3) require that, once this has been established, the prosecution must prove that the way in which the company's activities were managed or organised by its senior management was a substantial element in the breach of the relevant duty of care.

Steven Berry, 45 years old, was employed as a maintenance worker at the company's Hyde factory. Parts – but not all – of the roof of the factory build-ing had been replaced in recent years leading up to the incident. At one end, an old part of the roof, consisting of roof panels made of translucent fibre-glass, had needed repairs from time to time, and the court heard evidence of holes being patched with strips of tape to stop rainwater leaking on to the works below. The judge emphatically resisted the prosecution's suggestion that the fact that the roof needed repairing was, somehow, contributory to the

19   *R v Lion Steel Equipment Ltd*, Manchester Crown Court, 20 July 2012 (unreported).
20   *R v P&O European Ferries (Dover) Ltd* [1991] 93 Cr App R 72.
21   *R v Cotswold Geotechnical (Holdings) Ltd* [2011] ALL ER (D) 100 (May).
22   See *R v Kite and OLL Ltd*, Winchester Crown Court, 8 December 1994 (unreported).

defendants' guilt and, indeed, emphasised in his remarks that the case, rather, was about whether the *method* of carrying out the maintenance was causative of Mr Berry's death, and the criminal responsibility attaching to the company for that death occurring. All it did was to explain why Mr Berry had been there at the time; for he had made his way on to the roof of the building on 29 May 2008 in order to attend to the holes through which rainwater leaked onto the floor below.

But Mr Berry was not trained as a roofer; the judge summed up the deceased's duties as that of a general maintenance man. He and another man, Mr Baines (who was not called as a witness) would carry out small repairs about the premises; but evidence was heard that, if they were in any doubt about their ability to carry them out, they were instructed to ask for independent external contractors to attend.

The court further heard evidence that, while Mr Berry was aloft with all his weight upon the roof, a fibreglass rooflight became detached from some of its fixings, twisted, and he fell 13 metres to the floor below, suffering fatal injuries.

The indictment originally contained five counts:

Count 1: corporate manslaughter against Lion Steel contrary to section 1 of the Corporate Manslaughter and Corporate Homicide Act 2007, alleging that, on 29 May 2008, the defendant '*being an organisation, namely a corporation, and because of the way in which the organisations' [sic] activities were managed or organised by its senior management, caused the death of ... Steven Berry by failing to ensure that a safe system of work was in place in respect of work undertaken at roof height, which failure amounted to a gross breach of a relevant duty of care owed by it, to the deceased*'.

Count 2 alleged common law manslaughter against three directors of the defendant company: Kevin Palliser, works manager at the Hyde factory; Richard Williams, works manager at Lion Steel's other factory in Chester; and Graham Coupe, the company's financial director.[23] It was the Crown's contention that each was under a personal duty of care towards the company's employee Mr Berry, and that he died as the result of what the Crown say was their gross negligence (the judge rather clarified the Crown's assertion as to the defendants' alleged gross breach of the duty of care, which the Crown argued was owed by them as directors to him as an employee).

---

23 The case of *R v Adomako* [1995] 1 AC 171 established the precedent for the jury to convict in a case of gross negligence manslaughter against an individual defendant if it is satisfied beyond reasonable doubt that the defendant owed a duty of care to the deceased; that he was in breach of that duty; the breach of duty was 'a substantial' cause of death (as refined by *R v O'Connor* [1997] Crim LR p16 CA); and the breach was so grossly negligent that the accused can be deemed to have had such disregard for the life of the deceased that it should be seen as criminal and deserving of punishment by the state.

Count 3 contained a statutory health and safety charge, alleging that Lion Steel failed to discharge a duty pursuant to section 2 of HSWA.[24] It alleged that as Mr Berry's employer, it failed to ensure so far as was reasonably practicable the safety of employees working at height.

Count 4 alleged that the three directors committed the offence of neglect, contrary to section 37 of HSWA. It alleged that the failure by Lion Steel in count 3 was attributable to their neglect.[25]

Count 5 alleged against Lion Steel that there was a contravention of the Work at Height Regulations 2005[26] (and therefore an offence was alleged under section 33 of HSWA) because no suitable and sufficient measures were taken to prevent, so far as was reasonably practicable, persons falling a distance likely to cause injury.

At a preliminary hearing, count 1 was severed from the main indictment, because of the critical need to distance proceedings under the 2007 Act against the company from proceedings against the individual directors under the common law. In the judge's words, '*it would have been difficult in the extreme to try it alongside the count of manslaughter against the three directors, for reasons connected with the fact that the Act is not retrospective*'. The key issue focused on the admissibility of evidence in count 1, against the company under the 2007 Act, but tending to address the guilt of the directors in count 2, referring to conduct occurring before the commencement of the 2007 Act. Moreover, there could be no question of liability of the directors under the 2007 Act.[27] He ruled that a joint trial would have required directions to the jury '*of baffling complexity, which directions would probably have been ineffective*'.

---

24 'It shall be the duty of every employer to ensure, so far as is reasonably practicable, the health, safety and welfare at work of all his employees. . . including (a) the provision and maintenance of plant and systems of work. . . (c) the provision of such information, instruction, training and supervision as is necessary to ensure, so far as is reasonably practicable, the health and safety at work of his employees. . . (d) so far as is reasonably practicable as regards any place of work under the employer's control, the maintenance of it in a condition that is safe and without risks to health and the provision and maintenance of means of access to and egress from it that are safe and without such risks; (e) the provision and maintenance of a working environment for his employees that is, so far as is reasonably practicable, safe, without risks to health, and adequate as regards facilities and arrangements for their welfare at work.'

25 Where an offence under any of the relevant statutory provisions committed by a body corporate is proved to have been committed with the consent or connivance of, or to have been attributable to any neglect on the part of, any director, manager, secretary or other similar officer of the body corporate or a person who was purporting to act in any such capacity, he as well as the body corporate shall be guilty of that offence and shall be liable to be proceeded against and punished accordingly.

26 SI 2005 No 735.

27 Section 18 expressly excludes secondary liability for the new offence, while paragraph A1(a) of the Sentencing Council Guidelines is even more concise in stating that the offence can be committed only by organisations and not by individuals see Sentencing Council, 2010, *Corporate Manslaughter & Health and Safety Offences Causing Death, Definitive Guideline*, Sentencing Guidelines Council, London.

The judge also stayed count 5. There was subsequently no appeal against any of these rulings.

The result was that a jury was sworn in to hear the trial of the three directors for manslaughter at common law and the statutory offence of neglect, and of Lion Steel for breach of the HSWA – a statute demanding entirely different criteria to those for securing a conviction under the 2007 Act, involving, as it does, strict liability rather than depending on proof of negligence. The trial of the company under the 2007 Act in count 1 would be heard subsequently.

Once the trial was under way against the directors, the Crown called its evidence on what had occurred, including the evidence it said showed gross negligence by the director defendants and that would also serve against the company. At the end of the prosecution case submissions were made on behalf of the directors; for the Crown, this is where the case started to unravel.

In a criminal prosecution under English law, the prosecution must establish that every element of the crime defined under the statute has been proved beyond reasonable doubt by the weight of the evidence adduced by the prosecution.[28] How persuasive the jury finds the evidence is entirely up to them, of course.

At the end of the prosecution case, if it is apparent that the evidence is insufficient to establish the elements of the crime, consisting of the mens rea and actus reus required by the statute, then it would be unsafe to direct the jury to reach a verdict on the evidence, and a submission can be made to the judge by the defence that there is no case to answer. Submissions are made to the judge in the jury's absence, for a consideration of the law is not within their remit.[29] All they need know is the substantive law that makes a persuasive case on the evidence that they hear. If, having heard the defence's submission and the prosecution's reply, the judge concludes that the prosecution evidence, taken at its highest, is such that a jury properly directed could not properly convict on it, it is his duty to stop the case. In that situation the jury must be directed to return a verdict of not guilty.[30]

That being said, generally it is not open to the judge to rule that there is no case to answer due to insufficient evidence before the close of the prosecution case, so that the judge can draw an informed opinion for himself in addition to the arguments established by the defence and the prosecution reply.

28 It would be fair to qualify this only in so far as strict liability offences, such as those in the HSWA, demand merely that the prosecution establish breach of health or safety provisions, which then places a reverse burden of proof on the defendant to show, on the balance of probabilities, that it had exercised due diligence.

29 *R v Falconer-Atlee* [1974] 58 Cr App R 348 CA.

30 *R v Galbraith (George Charles)* [1981] 2 All ER 1060; [1981] 73 Cr App R 124; [1981] Crim L R 648.

In *R v Brown*[31] it was confirmed that if, at any time after the conclusion of the prosecution case, the judge is satisfied that no jury, if properly directed, could convict, he has the power to withdraw the case from the jury, but that this is a power to be sparingly exercised. That being said, this is precisely what happened in the trial against P&O Ferries for corporate manslaughter in the case of the *Herald of Free Enterprise*.[32] For those commentators baying for a conviction under the 2007 Act, this would be a disaster surpassed only by a not guilty verdict.

On 2 July 2012, the judge duly ruled that in the cases of two directors of Lion Steel (Richard Williams and Graham Coupe) there was no case to answer on the common law manslaughter count, and in the case of Mr Williams also no case to answer on the count of neglect. In the judge's opinion, the case against them should never have been brought and he was minded to direct the jury to acquit them; interestingly, however, the combined effect of sections 1 and 18 of the 2007 Act expressly exclude a director's personal liability for the new offence, whether on an individual basis or on the basis that they aided, abetted, counselled or procured it.

As a result, any personal conviction or acquittal would have been on an indictment for manslaughter and, as such, would have been immaterial to the company itself, save for the probative value of evidence that would have been admissible both under common law and the statute. The judge did feel that the prosecution had an arguable, albeit weak, case against the director Mr Coupe but the merit of that case disappeared as the evidence in the case unfolded and there just remained a case on neglect.

It is apparent that, in the light of this, the prosecution and defence negotiated a solution with acceptable pleas that would bring the trial to a close before the case against Lion Steel was due to commence. As a result of the negotiation, Lion Steel then pleaded guilty to the count alleging corporate manslaughter, and the prosecution offered no evidence against the directors on the remaining counts.

The personal priorities of the directors to eliminate the risk of conviction and imprisonment of manslaughter had been met, but the downstream consequence is that we are none the wiser, nor are we better informed, as to whether the 2007 Act will succeed in its task of securing corporate accountability for manslaughter where its common law predecessor had failed.

The exercise was not entirely a waste of time, though. The judge made some notable observations, which can be employed to clarify some key points in the prosecution of a company under the 2007 Act.

---

31   *R v Brown (Davina)* [2002] 1 Cr App R 5 CA.
32   *R v P&O European Ferries (Dover) Ltd* [1991] 93 Cr App R 72.

It will be recalled that section 1 of the 2007 Act renders the company guilty if the way in which its activities were managed or organised (a) caused the victim's death and (b) amounted to a gross breach of a relevant duty of care owed by the company to the deceased. The demands of section 1(3) require that, once this had been established, the prosecution must prove that the way in which the company's activities were managed or organised by its senior management was a substantial element in the breach of the relevant duty of care.

With the thoroughness perhaps not altogether ubiquitous in Crown Court proceedings, it has been extremely helpful that the judge should have addressed his sentencing remarks in the case with minute care.[33] In corporate manslaughter the Sentencing Guidelines demand nothing less, although not for the purpose of divining the emerging law but, in this case, the judge was clarifying his decision on a submission on the admissibility of evidence under that law, as will be seen. The judge assessed the risk of a fall through the roof as an obvious one, and he felt that the company's management team – that is, those senior persons responsible for making decisions about how the whole or a substantial part of its activities are to be managed or organised, or the actual managing or organising of the whole or a substantial part of those activities, as provided in the Act[34] – should have appreciated it. The judge accepted evidence that a Health and Safety Executive (HSE) inspector had conducted an inspection in 2006 and warned Lion Steel that warning notices should be erected to keep persons away from fragile roofs, and referred to HSE guidance and codes of practice warning of the danger of fragile roofs, and emphasising the need for proper supervision and training.

The judge accepted evidence that Lion Steel had, in fact, responded to this risk by devising a safe system of work, intending to keep Mr Berry off the fragile areas. What, he felt, it had not done, was to train him properly, or to equip him or others with equipment, in the form of a harness and line, which would protect him should an accident occur. Without catwalks or barriers defining safe access routes, the judge concluded that there was nothing to discourage a workman from taking a shortcut if he carelessly chose to do so, echoing the words of Mr Justice Bridge in a judgment against the Blue Star Line when he observed:

> . . . *it is not only the reasonable behaviour of employees which it is an employer's duty to anticipate; it may include unreasonable behaviour.*[35]

---

33 For the sentencing remarks see http://www.judiciary.gov.uk/media/judgments/2012/r-v-steel-equip-ltd-sentencing-remarks.

34 Section 1(4).

35 *Chalmers v Blue Star Line Ltd* [1968] 1 Ll R 643.

Two questions need to be addressed in order to reach the core of the problem of establishing guilt in this case:

1   Whether the system adequately managed the risk which was reasonably foreseeable that Mr Berry was working on and around the fragile roof with no precautions or training.
2   If the management had failed for this reason, was the resultant breach so sufficiently gross as to amount to a crime?

Much of the argument in the case crucially revolved around the admissibility of evidence that came into existence before the 2007 Act entered into force;[36] this was an issue that, however important to the case in question, would not likely be shared by cases in the future and, so, it is not intended to review the point in this work.

The judge drew attention to the Act's reliance on the application of the common law of negligence,[37] without dwelling on the old baggage that accompanies the application of civil liability to a criminal offence.[38] Whatever the argument on admissibility, the judge brought into sharp focus the key point that the prosecution still had to meet the demands of section 1(3), which states that the company would only be guilty '*if the way in which its activities are managed or organised by its senior management is a substantial element in the breach*'.[39] This hurdle being cleared, the prosecution would then have to show that the breach of the relevant duty of care would have to be 'gross', defined by section 1(4) as conduct that '*falls far below what can reasonably be expected of the organisation in the circumstances*'.

The decision on what constitutes a gross breach of duty is a matter reserved for the jury in every case, but section 8 gives guidance on factors that the jury should consider. This section states inter alia:

> *The jury must consider whether the evidence shows that the organisation failed to comply with any health and safety legislation that relates to the alleged breach, and if so, (a) how serious that failure was and (b) how much of a risk of death it posed.*

---

36   Paradoxically, had the defendant been arraigned under the common law charge, the problem for the prosecution would not have arisen, but such an option was not open to them, because section 20 states that '*The common law offence of manslaughter by gross negligence is abolished in its application to corporations, and in any application it has to other organisations to which section 1 applies.*'
37   Paragraph 21 of the explanatory notes to the Act clarifies that section 2(1) requires the duty of care to be one that is owed under the law of negligence. This will commonly be a duty owed at common law.
38   See *Corporate Manslaughter: New Horizon of False Dawn?* for a detailed argument.
39   Section 1(3).

Even given any perceived weakness in the prosecution case arising out of the evidence predating the Act, the judge expressed a leaning towards the interpretation in this case that

> *a breach may be considered as gross in late April 2008 because (for example) it consisted of a failure at that time to act on knowledge gained long before.*

5.6 The *JMW Farm* case

In fact, the much-heralded case of Lion Steel was preceded by a matter of weeks by a prosecution in Belfast Crown Court, when the Recorder of Belfast, His Honour Judge Burgess, sentenced J M W Farm Limited for the corporate manslaughter of Robert Wilson, one of the company's employees, who, on 15 November 2010, was washing the inside of a large metal bin that was positioned on the forks of a forklift truck. In a seemingly Heath-Robinson arrangement, such a method of cleaning was by no means unique, for the positions of the forks on the usual truck corresponded with the position of the sleeves on the bin, giving an apparently safe foundation for the process; but this truck was not the normal one, having replaced it when the normal truck had gone for servicing a number of weeks earlier. As a result, the arrangement was now decidedly unstable and, with the inevitability of Greek tragedy, when he jumped onto the side of the bin it overbalanced and, when he fell to the ground, the bin fell on top of him, killing him.

In this case, the defendant company also pleaded guilty and, so the 2007 Act was not tested before a jury. Once again, though, we may hazard some analysis of the evidence as applied to the statutory provisions. The court was told that the company was aware of such a danger, having carried out a risk assessment that included instructions for anyone operating the forklift truck. But it is clear from the judge's remarks that this assessment had been made of the former truck; when it was replaced by the temporary truck, no assessment was made of the position of the forks relative to the sleeves on the bin. The judge commented that it would have been apparent to any operator that it would not be possible to take the necessary steps to secure against the foreseeable dangers and added that it was of particular concern that the operation had been going on from when the replacement forklift truck was deployed and the incident was not an isolated event. The judge concluded with rather wearied words that, yet again, the court was confronted with an incident '*where common sense would have shown that a simple, reasonable and effective solution would have been available to prevent this tragedy*'.[40]

---

40 *R v J M W Farm Limited*, Belfast Crown Court, 8 May 2012 (currently unreported). For the summary of judgment See: www.courtsni.gov.uk/en-GB/Judicial%20Decisions/SummaryJudgments/Documents/Summary%20of%20judgment%20-%20R%20v%20J%20M%20W%20Farm%20Limited/j_sj_R-v-JMW-Farm-Limited_080512.pdf.

In both cases, the judges relied heavily on the guidelines published by the Sentencing Guidelines Council in February 2010.[41] This gives us further assistance because of the commentary that necessarily defines the obligation on the prosecution to prove each of the elements beyond reasonable doubt, within the statutory limitations, establishing that the offence:

(a)   can be committed only by organisations and not by individuals;
(b)   has as its root element in a breach of a duty of care under the law of negligence;
(c)   requires that the breach be a gross breach, that is to say one where the conduct falls far below what can reasonably be expected of the organisation;
(d)   further requires that a substantial element in the breach is the way in which the organisation's activities are managed or organised by its senior management;
(e)   is committed only where death is shown to have been caused by the gross breach of duty.

In the *JMW Farm* case, the judge recited the court's function in a slightly different way to that summarised by Judge Gilbart in *Lion Steel*, stating that the court should firstly consider the seriousness of the offence by asking how foreseeable was serious injury; how far short of the applicable standard did the defendants fall; how common was a breach of this kind in the organisation; and how far up the organisation the breach went. The court was then required to consider both aggravating and mitigating factors. In this case the judge held that it was clearly foreseeable that the failure to address the hazard would lead to serious injury and indeed that the consequences could well be fatal; that the company had fallen far short of the standard expected in relation to such an operation; and that the operation was permitted to continue for some time. The judge added, however, that there was no evidence that this represented a systemic departure from good practice across the company's operations. This, itself, would lead us into some difficulty in reconciling the judgment with the Act. The Sentencing Guidelines Council particularly distinguishes guilt in corporate manslaughter cases from guilt in cases under the HSWA:

> *because corporate manslaughter involves both a gross breach of duty of care and senior management failings as a substantial element in that breach, those cases will generally involve systemic failures; by contrast health and safety offences are committed*

41   Indeed, in sentencing the defendant in such a case, the court is obliged to follow any sentencing guidelines, unless the court is satisfied that it would be contrary to the interests of justice to do so, pursuant to section 125 of the Coroners and Justice Act 2009. The 2010 Guidelines were updated in 2015.

whenever the defendant cannot show that it was not reasonably practicable to avoid a risk of injury or lack of safety; that may mean that the failing is at an operational rather than systemic level and can mean in some cases that there has been only a very limited falling below the standard of reasonable practicability.[42]

5.7 Where do we go from here?

As a result, we were left in rather a quandary: in the case against Lion Steel, the judge apparently had satisfied himself that there had been a systemic failure, from which (had the trial proceeded) it would have been safe for the jury to conclude that the breach was a significant (if not necessarily the only) cause of death; hence the essential elements of an offence under section 1 of the 2007 Act would be established. If, however, we analyse the judge's conclusion in *JMW Farm*, the rationale of his decision is equivocal; if there were no evidence of a systemic management failure, then it would not have been safe to leave the matter for the jury to decide and a guilty verdict would be misconceived.

---

42 Paragraph A(4).

6 The Corporate Manslaughter Act – Critical review by case study

6.1 The future came and went in the mildly discouraging way that futures do[1]

Following the halting success of the prosecution in *Lion Steel*, there was much speculation that the number of prosecutions would rise dramatically. Indeed, according to research by solicitors Pinsent Masons, the number of new corporate manslaughter cases opened by the Crown Prosecution Service rose from 45 in 2011 to 63 in 2012 – an increase of 40 per cent, with 141 corporate manslaughter cases opened since records began in 2009 and 56 cases currently being investigated for prosecution. The CPS has not readily disclosed such statistical information on its website, and one is left wondering when the next case will be revealed, and lead, one way or the other, to a more definitive conclusion on the ability of the 2007 Act to deliver what the common law offence of corporate manslaughter did not.

In this chapter we will look at some of the cases that have been heard to date under the 2007 Act. It is emphatically not an exhaustive review of all the cases, primarily because, with every new case that comes to court, this work would become progressively more historic and out of date. In these case studies we will form a view as to how the 2007 Act is working, so that we can then apply it to the maritime and civil aviation sectors, which will enable us to draw conclusions on how the industry must plan its risk management to avoid corporate accountability.

6.2 *R v J Murray & Son Limited*

In October 2013 the case against J Murray & Son Limited[2] was heard in the Crown Court in Northern Ireland. But this was not a trial in which the jury was required to wrestle with the evidence in order to return a verdict under

---

1 Neil Gaiman, *Good Omens.*
2 Case number [2013] NICC 15.

the statute, for the company had pleaded guilty. And so the judge made out the argument on liability for them.

The defendant company was a small rural business, part of whose work involved mixing animal feed for local farms. On 28 February 2012, 47-year-old Norman Porter, described as a 'casual worker', was working at or near a meal mixer used for making animal feed, and putting in the ingredients from the top when he fell in, and suffered an appalling death. The working method had been devised by Daniel James Murray, who, in the judge's words, had been '*effectively the controlling director of the company*'. The judge may have been unwise to employ jargon that harked back to the days of the common law offence of corporate manslaughter, before the inception of the Act, as this might imply a reliance upon old tests that Parliament had wanted to sweep away for their unreliability in obtaining convictions.

The judge went on to describe the factory process, which involved delivering ingredients into the mixer through the top of the machine, for which sections of the upper metal protective covering had been removed, exposing the operator to the risk of harm from moving parts within the mixer.

The judge addressed the management failure by noting the opinion of expert evidence that the risk of harm could have been averted by a modification to render it safe for filling from the top if the panels had been replaced by a feed hopper that guarded an operator from the working parts, for a cost of £5,000 or '*probably rather less than that if manufactured and fitted by a local tradesman*'.[3]

There was no eye-witness evidence of the fatal accident but the judge stated:

> *It was plainly entirely foreseeable, indeed obvious, that a person either deliberately or accidentally entering the danger zone of the machine would meet with serious injury or death. During the course of his subsequent police interviews Mr Murray was asked whether he appreciated that after the top panels had been removed something might have fallen into the machine to which he replied '. . . that machine was as safe as a row of houses for me working and anybody working and I don't know what happened that day'.*

The judge disagreed with Mr Murray's assessment and concluded with a summary of all the constituent features that define liability for gross negligence manslaughter:

- The duty of care owed to the deceased was broken by a system of work that was '*anything but safe*'.

---

3   The judge's own words.

- The death was entirely attributable to the breach of the duty of care – yet again stating '*at its highest level of direction*'.
- It was an '*obvious and gross breach of the duty of care owed by the company to the deceased whose very grave potential consequences ought to have been plainly obvious to Mr Murray had he given them a moment's thought*'.

Whichever way the case was regarded, though, the inescapable truth was that the defendant company had pleaded guilty and, subsequently, the charge of unlawful killing on which the director Mr Murray was charged was not proceeded with. The judge was alive to the importance of this case in the history of the new 2007 Act, and was undeterred by the plea of guilty in setting out the necessary features that would have established guilt in a trial:

> *In assessing the seriousness of the offence I have taken account of the following matters while bearing in mind throughout that by its plea of guilty the company must be taken to have accepted the statutory ingredients of the offence to include implicit admissions that the breach here was gross, that is to say one where the conduct fell far below what could reasonably have been expected, and that a substantial element in the breach was the way in which the fatal activity had been managed by the senior management in the person of Mr Murray.*

- *How foreseeable was serious injury?*
  As discussed earlier, I consider the risk of serious injury was obvious.
- *How far short of the applicable standard did the defendant fall?*
  In my view it fell far short.
- *How common is this kind of breach in the company?*
  As noted above, this is the company's first known breach of Health and Safety requirements.
- *How far up the organisation did the breach go?*
  It went to the very top.

The company was sentenced with a fine of £100,000.[4]

But, once again, there was no issue on the facts to be tried by a jury.

6.3 *R v Princes Sporting Club Limited*

One month later, the case against Princes Sporting Club was heard at Southwark Crown Court, for the death by corporate manslaughter of 11-year-old Mari-Simon Cronje, who was killed after collision with a boat's propeller when she

---

4 The fine was to be paid in five annual instalments of £20,000 on 1 December 2013 and on the same date in each of the years 2014, 2015, 2016 and 2017.

fell from an inflatable banana boat ride. Once again, this was a guilty plea, but for us the case has special significance for the maritime industry because of the many and varied waterborne delights offered to passengers on cruises, and the facts deserve reporting in some detail.

Of particular note is the fact that this casualty was investigated by the Marine Accident Investigation Branch.[5] On 11 September 2010, Mari-Simon was among a group of ten children accompanied by four parents at the Princes Club water park, for a party which was to consist of two hours of wake boarding and knee boarding on Princes Club's cable ski lake and one hour riding on a towed inflatable banana. The weather conditions were good with little wind and mainly sunny skies. After initial booking in, the group were shown a safety video, which explained the procedures and safe use of the cable ski equipment, but did not include any safety instructions or guidance for the banana boat ride.

After the safety video the group went to the safety equipment store, where they were issued with a hard helmet, wetsuit and buoyancy aid.

Just before 15.30, the driver of the ski boat that was scheduled to tow the banana boat went to where the inflatable was stored, put it in the water and towed it to a lake known as Back Lake where the ride was to take place. The driver noted that one chamber of the banana boat was slightly under inflated but did not consider it necessary to add any air. The driver tied up the ski boat and the trailing banana boat to the jetty while the children went to the equipment room to exchange their hard helmets for the soft foam helmets that Princes Club insisted were worn when riding on the banana boat. It was recognised by the club that during a banana boat ride there was a risk that riders could fall against each other, and that if someone was hit by a fellow rider who was wearing a hard helmet the injury would be worse than if they were wearing a soft helmet. Only ten children were issued soft helmets as this was the maximum number of riders that were permitted to ride the banana boat at any one time. The driver did not give any safety instructions. An observer or spotter is a person nominated to sit alongside the ski boat driver (usually on the rearward-facing seat) to watch the tow and to relay any information concerning it to the driver, thus allowing him to concentrate on navigation and the water ahead.

At approximately 16.40, while they were under way Mari-Simon Cronje fell off the banana boat about 10 to 15 metres from the shore, but went unnoticed by the driver, who continued on a tight, roughly circular track. The watching parents, who were sitting at picnic tables near to the jetty, realised that the boat was not slowing and they began to shout and wave to attract the driver's

---

5   The facts and conclusions are extracted from the full report; see https://assets.digital.cabinet-office. gov.uk/media/547c6fa9e5274a4290000041/PrincesClubReport.pdf.

attention. Their efforts were not seen by the driver, and trials conducted after the accident found that it was not possible for someone in the boat to hear an adult shouting from the shore over the noise of the engine when the boat was more than 10 metres away. The boat ran over Mari-Simon, its propeller causing severe leg and perineal injuries. The driver realised what had happened, stopped the boat and then moved it to the nearby jetty, where he tied it up. One child jumped off the banana and swam to her friend's aid. Mari-Simon acknowledged her friend but soon lost consciousness. At the same time, the father of one of the children dived in to the water and swam the estimated 10 to 15 metres to reach Mari-Simon. He soon became aware of the severity of her injuries and cleared all of the children away from the scene and directed the driver to call the emergency services. He then managed to lift Mari-Simon on to the ski boat's aft boarding platform; the second father climbed into the boat and leant over the back seat to assist. The two men continuously carried out cardio-pulmonary resuscitation, one of them remaining in contact with the ambulance service operator, feeding back information when he was able to do so.

Shortly after 17.00 the emergency response services commenced administering medical treatment. Additional emergency vehicles, paramedics and doctors arrived and a medical helicopter landed near to the main entrance to the park to stand by to airlift Mari-Simon to hospital. At 17.39, the medical teams transferred Mari-Simon by road ambulance the short journey to the West Middlesex Hospital, Isleworth. Despite extensive attempts to revive her, Mari-Simon did not regain consciousness and she was declared dead at 18.22.

The report summarised the safety issues upon which it made its recommendations:

- Mari-Simon was not seen to fall in the water because an observer or spotter was not used on the ski boat.
- Her chances of being seen were decreased because of the low visibility equipment issued to her.
- Control measures are required to protect people in the water from the hazards of rotating propellers.
- The slower speed required when towing an inflatable compared to conventional water skiing, gave the ski boat a large bow-up trim that severely restricted the driver's forward visibility.
- The shorter route taken by the driver limited the time available to see Mari-Simon in the water.
- The process for completing the risk assessments was flawed and the risk assessment for the banana boat ride did not identify the hazard of a fallen rider not being spotted by the driver.

In addition the report summarised other safety issues that had been revealed in their investigation:

- Princes Club did not have a suitable communications system to cover the park.
- Princes Club had not prepared for an emergency such as a major injury on one of its lakes.
- Princes Club staff were not fully apprised of the club's risk assessments.
- Princes Club's health and safety management system was not being used correctly and this was not brought to the attention of its senior management by MHL, the health and safety consultant, during or following its site visits.
- It was unrealistic for the MHL consultant to carry out a full site inspection in the few hours that were available, or for Princes Club to expect that this service would meet its safety management needs.
- The person nominated to be the club's health and safety liaison officer had no specialist knowledge of the activities and there were no arrangements for her to be supported by anyone with such specialist knowledge.
- The lack of external oversight of towed inflatable rides meant that Princes Club's procedures went unchecked and there was no assurance in this case that the operation was being managed safely.
- Clarification is needed regarding the licensing of ski boats and banana boat rides.
- An appropriate, nationally recognised qualification, would help ensure ski boat/inflatable drivers are trained and competent to perform the task.
- The difficulties in bringing towed inflatable rides under existing licensing requirements could be overcome by local authorities using the 1907 Public Health Act to issue licences to operate.

Such evidence of a management failure was, undoubtedly, compelling, and the defendant company was accountable, but it was already in voluntary liquidation. His Honour Judge McCreath was more laconic than Judge Weir in the previous case, but chillingly for any company, he made the point that it matters not to a criminal court whether the defendant would be able to pay the fine imposed:

> *I propose to fine this defendant company every penny that it has. I have no power to do anything other than impose a fine and I can impose no more than all of its assets. I should say that if matters had been otherwise (the company had been trading or otherwise), that this is certainly a case where I would have given a fine which would have put it out of business.*

He sentenced the defendant with a fine of £134,579.69.

6.4 *R v P S & J E Ward Limited*

The trial was heard in Norwich Crown Court in 2014, on an indictment for corporate manslaughter, after their employee, tractor driver Grzegorz Krystian Pieton, 26 years old, was electrocuted when the metal hydraulic lift trailer he was towing hit an overhead power cable in July 2010.

After the trailer hit the cable, Pieton climbed out of the cab of his tractor and, when he touched the ground, he earthed the current that was now running through the vehicle. A member of the public spotted smoke coming from the tractor and called an ambulance after finding Pieton on the ground, but he died the same day.

Reasons for acquittal may have included the fact that an investigation by Norfolk police and the HSE found that, the day before the incident, one of the company's directors, Peter Ward, had taken the trailer to the field and performed the same task. There was no evidence Pieton (the employee killed) was following instructions from Ward when he repeated the task. He appears to have acted on his own initiative. The prosecution also alleged Pieton was not trained to work under power lines but during the trial it emerged he had attended a training course for forklift truck drivers that covered working under live cables.

The prosecution called the inspector who had conducted the investigation, who gave evidence that Pieton had driven the tractor and trailer, filled with soil from cleaned bulbs, into a flower field at a site owned by the defendant company, as part of his task to fill in an uneven path that had been damaged by work to lay irrigation pipes. But the court further heard that, the day before, one of the company's directors, Peter Ward, had taken the trailer to the field and performed the same task, without incident. But there was no evidence that Pieton was following instructions from Ward when he repeated the task. Indeed, the jury heard that the deceased had acted on his own initiative.

The weakness in this case was that the prosecution could not meet the absolute demand that all the elements of the actus reus and mens rea were proved beyond reasonable doubt, in particular, that the way in which the company's activities were managed or organised by its senior management was a substantial element in causing Pieton's death by a gross breach of a relevant duty of care owed by the organisation to the deceased. The weakness was highlighted by the fact that the prosecution had not arraigned a director or senior manager on any charge that could amount to evidence of such a breach. And so the seed of the prosecution's failure had been sown.

The prosecution also alleged Pieton was not trained to work under power lines. This would have been a clear breach of health and safety regulations; but as evidence of a management failure occasioning negligence it would have been more difficult to establish without other evidence. In the event, evidence was heard that he had attended a training course for forklift truck drivers that covered working under live cables. The prosecution case was becoming weak.

The joint police and Health and Safety Executive investigation also found that the company had only conducted a general risk assessment for work in the field. It said workers should be aware of power lines but did not provide details about how to work safely near them and there was nothing specific about tipping the trailer in that field, and that, furthermore, the defendant company had failed to provide workers with a plan showing the location of the power lines.

After a 12-day trial, the company was acquitted of corporate manslaughter.[6] Most importantly, it demonstrated that, without establishing that a senior management was guilty of gross negligence manslaughter, a jury would not likely be persuaded that there was sufficient evidence for a conviction against a defendant company for corporate manslaughter.[7]

6.5 R v Mobile Sweepers (Reading) Limited

This case perpetuates a thread running through corporate accountability that highlights a danger that the Marine Accident Investigation Branch has emphasised for many years, namely the risks attached to complacency, especially complacency in the face of some dangerous improvisation that is intended to meet some task outcome. It also conveniently underlines the court's power to punish, whether or not such punishment would render the company penniless.

In March 2014 the trial took place in Winchester Crown Court against Mobile Sweepers (Reading) Limited for the corporate manslaughter of Malcolm Hinton who died at Riddings Farm on 6 March 2012, after working on a repair underneath a road-sweeping truck at Mobile Sweepers. This time, evidence of a management failure was sought in the arraignment of the company's sole director, Mervyn Owens, who was charged with gross negligence manslaughter.

On 6 March 2002, one of the company's employees, Malcolm Hinton, was crushed to death as he carried out repairs to a road sweeper. The resultant investigation found that a prop, which was designed to support the weight of a hopper when it was raised in the tipping position, could not be used because of the poor condition of the vehicle. As a result, when Mr Hinton inadvertently removed a hose being used, the hopper fell backwards to the main chassis of the vehicle and crushed him as he worked underneath.

The company pleaded guilty to corporate manslaughter. In sentencing the company, His Honour Judge Boney said that the management failure was '*the*

---

6   It was found guilty of breaching section 2(1) of the Health and Safety at Work etc Act, for which he fined them £50,000 plus costs – which amounted to just £2,000 less than the fine itself.

7   The jury did, however, return a verdict of guilty for the lesser, statutory health and safety offence of failing to protect a worker.

most serious of its kind the Court is ever likely to hear' and accordingly fined the company all it had to pay. But the company had £12,000 left in the bank, which led the judge to order £8,000, the lowest fine yet ordered in a corporate manslaughter case, and a further order was made for £4,000 costs, wiping out the sum standing to credit in the company's bank account.

The company's sole director, Mervyn Ownes, pleaded not guilty to the charge of gross negligence manslaughter and an offence under Reg 5(1) of the Provision and Use of Work Equipment Regulations, but pleaded guilty to an offence under section 2 of the HSWA. The gross negligence manslaughter charge and the offence under the Provision and Use of Work Equipment Regulations were left to lie on file but the director pleaded guilty to the HSWA offence and was fined £183,000 plus £8,000 costs and was disqualified as a director for five years.

6.6 *R v Sterecycle (Rotherham) Limited*

This case illustrates another facet of the prosecution of offences, which takes further the judge's comments in *Mobile Sweepers*, and leads us to question just how valid is it to pursue a case in corporate manslaughter, when the defendant company has already gone out of business. The trial took place in Sheffield Crown Court in November 2014, when the defendant company answered a charge of corporate manslaughter, with additional charges against three managers – not directors in this case – under section 7 of the HSWA, which naturally was intended to establish the evidence for the management failure.

The defendant company's activities involved waste disposal, and it was developing a prototype system for dealing with general household waste involving a large autoclave that could deal with 24 tonnes of rubbish at a time. The seal on a door failed, leading to an explosion of steam in which one employee was killed and another seriously injured. Examination of the debris revealed that the door-locking mechanism had been damaged prior to the explosion. There was evidence that maintenance was inadequate, and that dangerous operating practices had been allowed to develop under commercial pressure to keep the plant in constant operation: the classic ingredients of a major industrial accident.

By the time the case came to trial the company was already in liquidation but the prosecution pursued the case nevertheless, and the company was convicted and fined £500,000. It might have proved a point to discourage management failures, but one questions whether it was in the public interest to spend money in this way. The Criminal Procedure Rules states that the overriding objective is that criminal cases be dealt with justly.[8] The question of cost–effectiveness

---

8 Rule 1.1 of the Criminal Procedure Rules 2015, SI 2015 No 1490.

of a trial is not addressed, but the Code for Crown Prosecutors, issued by the DPP under section 10 of the Prosecution of Offences Act 1985, gives guidance to prosecutors on the general principles to be applied when making decisions about prosecutions. Code 4.1 defines two stages of the test: (i) the evidential stage; followed by (ii) the public interest stage. If satisfied that there is sufficient evidence to put to a jury upon which it could safely return a verdict beyond reasonable doubt, then it must consider whether it is in the public interest to proceed. In this context they should consider whether prosecution is proportionate to the likely outcome, and in so doing they must consider, among other things,

> *The cost to the CPS prosecution service and the wider criminal justice system, especially where it could be regarded as excessive when weighed against any likely penalty ... but cost is a relevant factor when making an overall assessment of the public interest.*

Moreover:

> *Cases should be capable of being prosecuted in a way that is consistent with principles of effective case management.*

It is therefore valid to question the balance of priorities that were weighed when the decision was taken to proceed to trial.

6.7 *R v MNS Mining Limited*

In 2014 the trial took at place at Swansea Crown Court of MNS Mining Ltd on an indictment containing four counts of corporate manslaughter.

On 15 September 2011 a serious accident happened at the Gleision Colliery, a drift mine in Port Talbot, north of Swansea, that had been operating since the 1960s. Seven miners were working a narrow seam and using explosives at the coal face. A routine blasting operation to extract coal took place at 09.21, but precipitated a sudden and unexpected inrush of 660,000 gallons of water that the explosion had released from adjacent disused mine workings. Garry Jenkins, Philip Hill, David Powell and Charles Breslin died, while the other three escaped, including the mine manager, Malcolm Fyfield, who was subsequently charged with four counts of gross negligence manslaughter. MSN Mining were charged with the corporate manslaughter of the deceased. As always, it was necessary that a senior manager be held liable for gross negligence manslaughter as evidence of the management failure that is so crucial to criminal liability under the 2007 Act.

The prosecution case against Mr Fyfield was founded on gross negligence manslaughter on the evidence that he was in breach of his duty by reason of failings under the Mines (Precautions Against Inrushes) Regulations 1979. Regulation 6 applies to:

> *Mine workings in potentially hazardous areas and provides that a working in a mine which would be within 45 metres of (i) the surface, (ii) any rock or stratum containing or likely to contain water . . . or 37 metres of any disused mine workings, shall not be carried out unless the manager . . . shall obtain sufficient information to enable him to consider whether an inrush . . . may occur if the working is carried on without taking precautionary measures.*

Paragraph 3 of Reg 6 provides further that '*If the manager is of the opinion that such an inrush will not occur he shall ensure that the working is not carried on unless he has given notice of the reasons for that opinion to the inspector for the district. . . . at least 30 days in advance or such shorter period in advance as the inspector may allow in any particular case*'.

The prosecution presented evidence that the mine plan showed blue water lines and the words '*Underground Water*'. It also showed that there were old mine workings surrounded by a green hatched precautionary zone, that should have alerted him to the requirements of the 1979 Regulations. The evidence of his own appraisal of the risk was offered in a black biro line that he had allegedly drawn on the plan to show a water line present in the old mine workings.

The corporate manslaughter case against the mining company was dependent, therefore, upon establishing that Mr Fyfield was guilty of a gross breach of his duty of care to the deceased as a result of his breaches of the regulations, which formed at least a substantial element of the management failure demanded by the 2007 Act.[9]

The jury heard evidence from a number of surveyors called by the prosecution who had personal knowledge of the mine; but they said that they had not physically surveyed the water levels in the mine and could not confirm the accuracy of the blue water lines, simply having transferred the markings from one plan to another. One surveyor gave evidence of how he marked green hatching around old workings, which were inaccessible so he was not able to confirm whether or not they contained any hazards including water. Clearly this was relevant to the green hatched areas on the plans before the jury, but it was then revealed that the use of green hatching to denote a precautionary zone

---

9 The author is grateful to Kennedys Law LLP for published information on this case. See www.kennedyslaw.com/files/Uploads/Documents/Health%20and%20Safety/Kennedys%20-%20Defending%20corporate%20manslaughter.pdf.

was not in accordance with the standard symbols set out in a code for guidance; this would not necessarily represent a warning to an experienced mine manager. Additional evidence was heard from mine managers called by the prosecution, none of whom could confirm the blue lines showed the accurate water levels, with one mine manager giving evidence to the contrary, saying that he had travelled regularly through the old workings, which had taken him some way below the blue line. The mine managers also gave evidence of other inaccuracies on the mine plan identifying large areas in the mine that had been worked but where the coal workings were not recorded.

At this stage, the question arises as to how the Crown Prosecution Service had satisfied itself that such evidence would have been satisfactory to prove guilt beyond reasonable doubt to a jury. Nevertheless, the case had continued to trial.

Of the many witnesses called by the prosecution, one was the lead inspector with responsibility for inspecting the mine. He honestly answered the questions put to him, and told the jury of Mr Fyfield's unblemished reputation and technical competence, describing him as the 'Alex Ferguson' of mine managers.

The jury also heard evidence that offered doubt about the reliability of the investigation process, including the surveys undertaken following the disaster, in particular regarding unrecorded workings, which, the defence argued, could have been the source of the inrush of water, but no survey was offered by the prosecution to ascertain the extent of the unrecorded workings identified in previous evidence. It was, of course, incumbent upon the prosecution to adduce all the necessary evidence upon which the jury could safely determine the defendant's guilt beyond reasonable doubt, and it would have been important, therefore, that the prosecution could satisfy the jury with such evidence; and when the defence argued that such areas of unrecorded mine workings could have been a source or route for the water involved in the inrush, the prosecution did not call any geological or hydrogeological evidence to assist the jury with what the potential causes of the inrush might have been.

It was not as if this turn of events would have taken the prosecution by surprise: in April 2012, the prosecution had obtained an initial expert opinion that there may be other hydrogeological factors that could have caused the inrush, making the prosecution theory just one of a number of alternatives.

By contrast, the defendant's evidence was compelling, putting in doubt the reliability of the prosecution case against him. He argued that the water involved in the inrush could not have been in the old workings for a prolonged period of time and that he approached the work safely. In rebutting particular aspects of the prosecution case, he discredited the applicability of the 1979 Regulations, which applied to 'disused' workings; the workings in question were accessible and, thus, fell out of the definition. To put the controversy of the green hatched areas on the plans to rest, he did not recognise the green hatched area to be a precautionary zone or to trigger the requirements under the Regulations – and, as we have seen, there was no statutory basis for them in the first place. His inspections and recent exploratory operations had not revealed anything more than a trickle of water entering the site. The black biro line he drew on the mine plan to denote the level of water in the old workings was made before he inspected the area – and he discounted it any way after he conducted his site inspection.

Such evidence persuaded the jury that there was no evidence of gross negligence, and Mr Fyfield was acquitted.

The case of corporate manslaughter now demanded other evidence of a management failure that proved to be a substantial cause of the fatal accident. The prosecution had not brought charges against the company under health and safety legislation, though, which meant that, in the absence of proof beyond reasonable doubt, the case against the mining company had to fail.

6.8 *R v CAV Aerospace Limited*

The facts of this case convey a scenario that will be familiar to many involved in personal injury litigation – and perhaps the sentence reflects the courts' concern with such familiarity. Any operation that sees in its normal business the loading, stowage, and moving of objects, large or small, will identify with the risks in this case.

The company is well described by the introduction in its own website:

> *CAV is a leading supplier of precision machined parts to the aerospace industry. With 600 employees and 33,500 sqm of manufacturing and distribution facilities (in both the UK and Poland) we design, manufacture, assemble and deliver components to leading aircraft manufacturers such as Airbus, Boeing and Gulfstream.*[10]

In the course of its operation, the company had stockpiled the metal sheets it required in its manufacturing processes. During the trial it was averred that the senior management of the company '*had received clear, unequivocal and repeated warnings*' of the hazard of such stockpiling over a sustained period of years, and understood that there were potentially disastrous consequences if nothing significant was done about this. The court heard that some of the most obvious solutions were rejected on cost grounds, though.

Paul Bowers had recently joined as an employee, when he was making his way down a designated safe walkway, past a stack of raw sheets of metal that had been piled dangerously high. The stack fell on top of him, and he died of his injuries.

10 www.cav-aerospace.com/.

The quantum of the fines in this cases was exceptional in the development of corporate manslaughter cases. Upon conviction, in July 2015 CAV Aerospace was fined £600,000 on the corporate manslaughter charge and £400,000 for breaching the HSWA; they also had to pay costs of £125,000.

6.9 *R v Linley Developments*

This case was concluded in September 2015, but has an inescapable resonance with the first successful prosecution under the 2007 Act in *R v Cotswold Geotech.* in 2011. Linley developments was a construction development business that employed 28-year-old Gareth Jones.

The court heard that, two days before the fatal accident, managing director Trevor Hyatt visited the site in St Albans, Hertfordshire, to find that the foundations for a store room under construction would leave the floor at a higher level than in the adjoining building. Project manager Alfred Baker suggested putting in a step but the client said he would prefer them at the same level, while two workers told Mr Hyatt that, if they were to dig lower, they might need to underpin the footing of the existing wall. He told them to dig to a lower level regardless.

On 30 January 2013, Gareth Jones, a sub-contracted employee, died instantly when a wall collapsed on him at the site. The investigation that led to the charges found:

- Linley Developments failed to carry out a risk assessment or create a method statement for the excavation.
- Linley Developments had not installed supports or buttresses to prevent the wall falling forward as the trench deepened.
- The wall was inherently unsafe because, during construction a year before, the foundations had not been bonded with it.

Linley Developments pleaded guilty to corporate manslaughter and was fined £200,000 and ordered to pay costs of £25,000. Yet another small company, it was allowed to pay the fine over six years.

Trevor Hyatt was sentenced to six months' imprisonment suspended for two years, after pleading guilty to breaching Regs 28 and 31 of the Construction (Design and Management) Regulations 2007. He was also fined £25,000 with £7,500 in costs. Judge Bright said he had considered disqualifying him as a director but '*did not believe it necessary, proportionate or just to do so*'. Alfred Barker, 59, of Gazeley, Suffolk was given a six-month prison sentence, suspended for two years, after pleading guilty to breaching Regs 28 and 31 of the same regulations. He was ordered to pay costs of £5,000.

6.10 *R v Maidstone and Tunbridge Wells NHS Trust*

This is arguably the most significant case since the 2007 Act came into force, because of the nature of the decision and its implication for gross negligence, in the light of the similarity of issues with the fundamental case of *R v Adomako*.

In October 2012 Frances Cappuccini was admitted to Tunbridge Wells Hospital in Pembury, Kent, when consultant anaesthetist Dr Errol Cornish acted in a caesarean section for the birth of her second child. Another anaesthetist, however, Dr Nadeem Azeez, had primary responsibility.

By the end of the operation Mrs Cappuccini had lost more than two litres of blood, although the baby had been delivered. She was subsequently operated on for a postpartum haemorrhage, but never woke up from the anaesthetic. She went into cardiac arrest just over three hours after the operation had finished on 9 October 2012, and died at 16.20.

After an investigation Dr Cornish was charged with gross negligence manslaughter, and the hospital trust was arraigned on an indictment for corporate manslaughter. Both pleaded not guilty. In the trial at Inner London Crown Court it emerged that Dr Nadeem Azeez was primarily responsible for Mrs Cappuccini's care, but did not face a trial alongside his co-defendants because he had returned to his native Pakistan.

The prosecution alleged that Azeez and Cornish failed in the elementary task of protecting her airway so that sufficient air reached Cappuccini's lungs as she recovered from the operation. The case alleged that if one or both doctors was found to be grossly negligent then the trust employed someone it knew or should have known was not suitably qualified or trained, which, they argued, would have satisfied the definition of criminal liability under section 1 of the 2007 Act.

At the end of the prosecution case, however, the defendants made a submission that the prosecution had offered insufficient evidence that could safely be put to the jury to reach a verdict on the indictment and, therefore, that there was no case to answer. The judge, Mr Justice Coulson, agreed and instructed the jury to acquit both defendants.

The judge took the view that there was no question that Frances Cappuccini should not have died at the trust hospital on 9 October, but identified a series of flaws in the prosecution case, including evidence that showed some of locum Dr Cornish's actions had been, in his words, '*about as far from a gross negligence manslaughter case as it is possible to be*'. He also dismissed some of the allegations against the trust as '*perverse*'.

It will be recalled that, in *R v Adomako*[11] the defendant was the anaesthetist during an eye operation on a patient, who had failed to notice that during the

---

11 *R v Adomako* [1995] 1 AC 171.

course of the operation the tube from the ventilator supplying oxygen to the patient had become disconnected for some six minutes, when the patient suffered a cardiac arrest, and subsequently died. At the trial for gross negligence manslaughter the judge directed the jury that the test to be applied was whether the defendant had been guilty of gross negligence, requiring that the prosecution had to satisfy them that the matters simply necessary to establish liability in the civil tort of negligence had been proved. The only factor which went beyond this level was that the facts had to persuade the jury that the negligence (or *incompetence* – the judge's word) of the accused *went beyond a mere matter of compensation and showed such disregard for the life and safety of others as to amount to a crime against the State and conduct deserving punishment.*[12]

The judge's observations on the application of civil liability massively outweigh that devoted to criminal liability; but, to summarise the principle in this case, the jury needs to consider whether:

- the defendant owed a duty of care to the deceased; and
- he was in breach of that duty; and
- the breach was so grossly negligent that it should be seen as criminal.[13] In other words, as Lord MacKay defined gross negligence at the appeal hearing, it depended:

> . . .*on the seriousness of the breach of the duty committed by the defendant in all the circumstances in which he was placed when it occurred and whether, having regard to the risk of death involved, the conduct of the defendant was so bad in all the circumstances as to amount in the jury's judgment*[14] *to a criminal act or omission.*[15]

The concept of criminal accountability for negligence has been consistently argued as a mischief that offends the principles of justice in criminal law. If it is the case that the mischief of criminal negligence is here to stay, then it is conceded that, in very real terms, *R v Adomako* lives, and must be applied to senior managers, because, of course, the mental element cannot be attributed to a corporate body, but those who manage it. This, therefore, is the strong rationale that can be determined as a result of the hospital trust case – which can give optimism for the defence case in future.

12   *R v Adomako* [1995] 1 AC 171.
13   In addition, the breach of duty was 'a substantial' cause of death; as refined by *R v O'Connor* [1997] Crim LR 16 (CA).
14   In this case, meaning the jury's conclusion.
15   *R v Adomako* [1995] 1 AC 171.

7 So near . . . the *Costa Concordia* disaster

7.1 The ship and her voyage

The *Costa Concordia* did not have a unique design model. The *Costa Fortuna*, 102,587 gross tons, which entered service in 2003, and her sister *Costa Magica*, which entered service in 2004, proved the design model that encouraged the owners Costa Crociere to place orders on a common design platform for five, nearly identical, twin sisters each grossing 114,140 tons, the first of which would be the *Costa Concordia*, which entered service in 2004. At full capacity she could carry 3,780 passengers and over 1,000 crew in all departments. The ship was launched in September 2005 and entered service in July of the following year. From her maiden voyage she maintained basically the same seven-day West Mediterranean cruise itinerary for her entire career, so her deck and engineering departments got to know the areas extremely well.

On her final voyage, the *Costa Concordia* had sailed from Civitavecchia, on 13 January 2012. Travelling at a speed of 15.5 knots, at 21.42 she struck rocks off the island of Giglio. She immediately veered sharply to the right, when, according to reports, the master continued to bring the ship around to starboard in a circle heading back toward the island. By this point the vessel was listing 20 degrees. The order to abandon ship was not given until 22.50. Expert evidence subsequently held that, had the order to leave the ship been given earlier all passengers should have been able to evacuate in less than an hour with the ship upright. Shortly before midnight, the list had increased to such a degree that the port lifeboats could no longer be lowered. Sometime between 22.30 and 23.40, Captain Schettino was reportedly seen getting into a lifeboat, although this was contradicted by Dominica Cemortan, described as a 25-year-old former hostess but reputedly a friend of Captain Schettino, who stated that she was on the bridge until 23.50, when the master told her to go to a lifeboat.

There were 3,216 passengers and 1,013 crew members aboard at the time she hit the rocks. Thirty-two passengers and crew died, 64 were injured. During the salvage operation, one member of the salvage team died.

7.2 Consequences

The Italian Ministry of Infrastructures and Transports has a department with the same investigative function in marine casualties as the UK's Marine Accident Investigation Branch of the Department of Transport. The Marine Casualties Investigative Body concluded its report with a number of findings that, however Delphic to readers, were completed in accordance with Italian law and, therefore, have valid authority in Italian sovereign jurisdiction.[1]

The overarching finding was that the root cause in the loss of the *Costa Concordia* was the '*human element*', the twenty-first century euphemism for human error:

> *It should be also noted that the Costa Concordia is, first of all, a tragedy, and that the 32 dead people and the 157 injured, depended only by the above mentioned human element, which shows poor proficiency by key crewmembers.*

Whether or not any individual should be blamed for such error should not form any basis for conclusion in the report. Of course in reality that depended on how the report was written.

Paragraph 5.1 of the report addressed navigation before the impact. The English version reflects the official translation, errors understood:

> *This is the phase of the incident is to be considered crucial to the investigation, as it is the cause of action originated the serious Concordia casualty, and in that sense is due firstly to highlight the conduct of the master geared wilfully to pass the ship in restricted waters and then in a small space, by a route parallel to and perpendicular to an excessively close to the shore, intervening in a very light way on the course (then with bows which gave the helmsman faculty of self-management) to generate a sweet turn, but at the same time very wide.*

The report identified some key constituent factors that were described as '*aggravating in his nautical behaviour*':

*   According to the evidence of the first officer, the master had difficulty reading the radar screen as he was not wearing his glasses for near vision.
*   The inappropriate application of ECDIS and radar.
*   The master was distracted by people on the bridge who were not part of the bridge team and had no good reason to be there, one of whom was making an external telephone call.

---

1   Ministry of Infrastructures and Transports Marine Casualties Investigative Body Cruise Ship Costa Concordia Marine casualty on 13 January 2012 Report on the safety technical investigation. Referred to *passim*.

- The navigational orders given by the master to the helmsman, aimed at providing the compass course to be followed instead of the rudder angle.

The investigating body did not find fault with the ship's safety management system delivered by the company under Code 5 of ISM but, rather, the way in which the bridge procedures were implemented, for which the master had full responsibility.[2]

In addition to the master's acts or omissions, the report condemned the whole bridge team:

> *The passive attitude of the staff (team) on the bridge is just as reprehensible, and neither the most authoritative of the Officers (1st Deck Officer,) resulted from the records to have ever urged the master to tighten/speed up the turn, nor gave him information about the imminent danger despite before the arrival of the master had strongly criticized the bridge the decision to follow a route so close to the shore, calling it a true madness. It can be criticized also, the missed employment of the bridge staff (3 officers) both during the phase in which the watch was kept by the 1st Deck Officer, both when the master took command . . . The present case demonstrates the inadequacy, in terms of organization and then about 'who does what' of the Bridge Team. In this second juncture the 1st Deck Officer, could have used the staff of the bridge for warning about the dangerous approaching), rather than simply repeat the orders of the master to the helmsman or changing the speed.*

In February 2015, Francesco Schettino was finally found guilty of manslaughter by the panel of three judges (there is no jury process in Italy) and sentenced to 16 years and one month in jail. But his case had been espoused by the Italian national consumer group Codacons, whose lawyer sought to shine the spotlight of suspicion upon the owners, stating there was '*an obvious causal link between them and numerous deaths*'. Other lawyers expressed discomfort with the distancing of the company from their master, by levelling the blame onto him, which resonated with controversial assertions about responsibility for reckless and officially unauthorised sail-by events in which cruise ships regularly carried out the manoeuvre for goodwill or publicity purposes. The company's chief executive had to respond to the assertions when he told an Italian parliamentary committee: '*we have to do them like everyone else because we are in a global competition*'. The frightful fiend treading close behind the company, of course, was the spectre of corporate manslaughter.

---

2 See ISM 5.1, for which the master's absolute authority is underpinned by 5.2.

7.3 The spectre in the shape of corporate manslaughter

Paradoxically, Italy has had statutory law for corporate manslaughter longer then the UK. The casualty took place in Italian sovereign territory and, so, in theory, the owners would be exposed to the risk of a corporate manslaughter case.

Under Italian Law 231, a company may be criminally liable if an employee who holds a position as representative or manager (in other words has an administrative, or executive position in the company), or who, if they are not directly employed by the company, is subject to the direction and supervision of a representative or manager, commits one or more crimes listed in Law 231, in their own interest or to the advantage of the company, unless the company adopted and effectively implemented a suitable Law 231 Compliance Programme before the crime was committed. The list specifically includes *'crimes against the person, among which manslaughter and serious accidental injuries committed in violation of the provision on health and safety in the workplace'*.

It would be necessary to establish that the company did not have sufficiently robust rules and procedures in place to avoid an employee causing death by negligence, although the basis of Roman law, which characterises the Italian system, differs from the adversarial process under English law, in that it requires an examining judge to determine whether, on the alleged facts, the essential elements of the codified law are present to demonstrate a breach.

Law 231 provides a defence if the company proves either that:

- the individual who committed the crime acted solely in their own interest or on behalf of third parties and not in the interest of the company; or
- the company had adopted effective and specific internal compliance measures. This would require the company to show that it had established and implemented effective internal control systems for the purposes of preventing offences, before any offence was committed, by implementing an adequate compliance programme tailored to the characteristics of the company and setting up a supervisory body properly vested with independent initiative and inspection powers.

In essence, however, it would then be dependent on the defendant company to show that they took all reasonable steps and exercised all due diligence to avoid committing the offence, if it were to be acquitted.

In this context, it is highly relevant that the chairman and chief executive officer of Costa Crociere, Pier Luigi Fosci, later stated that the company's shore office was in touch with the ship at 22.05 but could not access the gravity of the situation because the master's conversation *'did not correspond to the truth'*. It was alleged that Captain Schettino reported problems but did not mention hitting rocks. At 22.12 the Italian coastguard contacted the ship after being alerted by calls from passengers to shore, but was told '*it's all okay, it's just a blackout, we're tak-ing care of the situation*'. By 22.30pm after a repeated call from the Coast Guard, the master agreed to send out a distress call. Twelve minutes later and exactly an hour after the collision, authorities were finally told that the problems began with striking the rocks.

The owners had corporate issues to confront as well as legal accountabil-ity. On the Monday following the foundering, the share value of Carnival Corporation & plc fell by over 20 per cent on the London Stock Exchange, representing a loss to the company of £1 billion. They recovered slightly to reach 17.04 per cent by the end of trading. On the following day, when the New York Exchange opened after Monday's public holiday, the stock value was down by 14.2 per cent. Carnival hastily assessed its financial risk and forecast that the casualty would likely reduce its earnings for the year 2012 by some-thing between $85 and $95 million, but could be as high as £100 million. The hull and machinery cover on the *Costa Concordia* carried a $30 million deductible, while their P & I cover for death and personal injury carried a $10 million deductible. Two major financial groups downgraded their ratings of Carnival stocks. As for the ship, she was not an actual loss, but the company no doubt questioned her future, as no passengers would likely book a cruise on her again, and which part of the Carnival group would want her on their balance sheet? The most likely scenario was that the insurers would declare her a total constructive loss.

In terms of the theory of their accountability under section 1 of the 2007 Act, it would be necessary for the prosecution to satisfy the jury beyond reasonable doubt that the owners were guilty in that the way their activities were managed or organised caused the deaths and amounted to a gross breach of a relevant duty of care owed by the owners to the deceased. In accordance with section 8, the jury must consider whether the evidence shows that the organisation failed to comply with any health and safety legislation that relates to the alleged breach and, if so, how serious the failure was, how much of a risk of death it posed, the extent to which the evidence shows that there were attitudes, policies, systems or accepted practices within the organisation that were likely to have encouraged any such failure, or to have produced tolerance of it, and, most fundamentally in the light of the cases that have been heard to date, have regard to any health and safety guidance that relates to the alleged breach. The relevant guidance is listed in subsection (5), which provides:

> *In this section 'health and safety guidance' means any code, guidance, manual or similar publication that is concerned with health and safety matters and is made or issued (under a statutory provision or otherwise) by an authority responsible for the enforcement of any health and safety legislation.*

This explains precisely why it has been so important to the prosecution to establish breaches under the HSWA or associated regulations.

7.4 What if. . . the admissibility of the Italian marine casualty investigation report in evidence

Of course, it is noteworthy that the evidence is factual, and the finding of an independent accident report has historically not been admissible in evidence in subsequent proceedings, and contains findings that are founded on the professional opinion of the investigators. The responsibilities of the Marine Accident Investigation Branch involve carrying out investigations to determine the causes of accidents at sea, publishing reports that include their recommendations on improving safety at sea, increasing awareness of how marine accidents happen, and improving national and international co-operation in marine accident investigations. Historically, a casualty report would not be used as evidence in proceedings; but a case in civil aviation changed all that. In the light of the findings of the *Costa Concordia* report, this could have very serious consequences indeed in the defence of criminal accountability.

The 2014 decision in *Hoyle v Rogers*[3] created a precedent that underlined the right of the trial judge to allow a statutory investigation report in evidence in proceedings. The rationale of the decision cannot be argued, because nobody can tell a judge what evidence they can or cannot rely on when managing their own proceedings, for that would interfere in the judge's inalienable right and obligation to manage a case justly.[4] As a result, though, by allowing the AAIB report arising out of the fatal accident giving rise to the civil claim under UK law in Part 32 of the Civil Procedure Rules, the report makers must be available for cross-examination otherwise the robustness of assertions of fact or opinion contained in the report would be undermined as unsafe. More relevantly in our hypothetical *Costa Concordia* prosecution, the conclusions drawn by the court from such evidence could lead to a finding of negligence in civil proceedings, which may subsequently underpin a decision to arraign a defendant on charges of criminal negligence and their employer for the corporate manslaughter arising out of the consequent management failure.

The inference is obvious, in that the very clear expressions of blame contained in the report in its conclusion in 5.1 identify the master as the 'villain of the

---

3 *Scott Hoyle v Julia Mary Rogers and Nicola Lucinda Rogers and Secretary of State for Transport (1st Intervener) and International Air Transport Association (2nd Intervener)* [2014] 3 WLR 148, [2014] CP Rep 30, [2014] EWCA Civ 257, [2014] 3 All ER 550.
4 Rule 1.1 of the Civil Procedure Rules defines the overriding objective of enabling the court to deal with cases justly.

piece', although it also lays blame on the bridge team as a whole. One paragraph of the findings is illustrative:

> . . . . *it is the cause of action originated the serious Concordia casualty, and in that sense is due firstly to highlight the conduct of the master geared wilfully to pass the ship in restricted waters and then in a small space, by a route parallel to and perpendicular to an excessively close to the shore, intervening in a very light way on the course (then with bows which gave the helmsman faculty of self-management) to generate a sweet turn, but at the same time very wide.*[5]

The authors of the report do not make reference to the owners, but it is the simplest step to take conclusions targeted against the master and apply the principles of liability for corporate manslaughter, to establish a prima facie case against them.

Paragraph 15 of the explanatory notes to section 1 of the UK's 2007 Act describes how the defendant owners must owe '*a relevant duty of care*' to the victim, and states:

> *The organisation must be in breach of that duty of care as a result of the way in which the activities of the organisation were managed or organised. This test is not linked to a particular level of management but considers how an activity was managed within the organisation as a whole. . . . an organisation cannot be convicted of the offence unless a substantial element of the breach lies in the way the senior management of the organisation managed or organised its activities. . . . The way in which the organisation's activities were managed or organised . . . . must have caused the victim's death. . . . The usual principles of causation in the criminal law will apply to determine this question. This means that the management failure need not have been the sole cause of death; it need only be a cause. . .*

A jury hearing the evidence of the statutory report in the *Costa Concordia* case may think just that.

---

5 Paragraph 5.1, official English translation.

8 Sentencing in corporate manslaughter

Domestic guidance, global consequence

8.1 The risk in globalisation

One of the constant features in shipping and aviation is the global nature of the business, which takes us beyond the sovereign jurisdiction of home states to territories where the normative ethics of societies see justice in quite different ways. When considering criminal negligence in fatal accidents, there is no better example of the extreme approach of justice than in the recent case of the *Sewol*.

On 16 April 2014, the South Korean flag ferry *Sewol* was on her scheduled run with 476 passengers and crew when she capsized with the loss of 304 lives, many of them school children.

The disaster produced an outpouring of grief and outrage after state prosecutors said the company ignored safety warnings and allowed the ship, which had been illegally redesigned, to be overloaded, The people's anger was aimed at the government, though, for allowing such a thing to happen at all, after it had given assurances that it would reduce bureaucratic procedures and improve emergency response. Additionally, the people of South Korea were looking for people to blame and hold criminally accountable, exactly as Victor Tadros has explained to us earlier in this work.[1] Within a month, the master, 69-year-old Captain Lee Joon-Seok was charged with homicide – in other words, murder, the maximum sentence for which was death. Three members of the crew were also charged with homicide, while the other 11 members of the crew were indicted for abandoning the ship.

An arrest warrant was also issued for Yoo Byung-eun, the 73-year-old owner; but he could not be found.

At the trial, the three judges held:

> *We find it hard to conclude that the defendants . . . were aware that all of the victims would die because of their actions and they had an intention to kill them. Therefore the murder charges are not accepted.*

---

1 Tadros, V (2006) 69(4) MLR 601–618, supra.

In Lee's defence, the court was invited to accept his apology for abandoning the passengers but that he could not have known that his actions would lead to the deaths of the victims. But, having been acquitted of homicide, Lee was found guilty of criminal negligence, and sentenced to 36 years' imprisonment. At the age of 70, it was likely that he would die in prison.

Authorities had launched a nationwide manhunt for the missing shipowner, Yoo Byung-eun, and raided a church compound owned by him, but they could not find him. His decomposed body was found in June in an orchard near his holiday home.

A South Korean court found that the owners routinely allowed the ferry to be overloaded, carrying more passengers than permitted, and signed off illegal renovations to increase its passenger capacity. On the occasion of the disaster, the investigation concluded the vessel was overloaded and serious defects would have been cause for detention, where renovations had made the structure of the ferry unstable and dangerous to proceed to sea.

The prosecution was bitter and acrimonious, hardly an environment in which the rules of natural justice could be followed, in which the tribunal was impartial and the defence would be heard in all aspects of the case against them. But it should not be thought that a fatal accident caused by a ship of any other flag would have been treated in any other way. As the master of the *Hebei Spirit* found after her grounding in South Korea in 2007, the state prosecutor would pursue a conviction relentlessly in order to achieve a prison sentence. Such is the character of the criminalisation phenomenon globally, and such is the fear that accompanies the process of sentencing.

Existing international law renders accountability by the flag state to the port state, and the accountability of the master to their flag state goes a long way to embracing the validity of a structure of law enforcement against a master by their flag state of its domestic laws as well as its international obligations, wherever the act or omission has taken place. In this context, however, we are left with the supreme difficulty in current law of the defective evolution of criminal negligence in the flag state's process of criminal accountability, let alone the application of criminal negligence in a port or coastal state where the people are demanding a scapegoat for the loss of life or damage to the environment.

To this extent, it may be argued that it matters not whether the hazard is confronted in a flag state or a port state court. Moreover, the mischief of inconsistency in the way in which evidence is managed and presented in the conflicting adversarial and inquisitorial systems, so long a barrier to the effective administration of criminal justice internationally, pales into insignificance when compared with the risk that it will be used to underpin an objective, rather than a subjective, test of the defendant's mens rea.

In this context the application of provisions under UNCLOS such as those in Articles 21 and 27, or, much more to the liking, no doubt, of the port state, the clear statement rule, so beloved in the priorities of the port state, would have little practical advantage or disadvantage to the master, while its preservation would, at least, meet the rights that inherently belong to state sovereignty in the judicial process, while conveniently disarming the port state's potentially inflammatory lack of confidence in the judicial process of the flag state concerned. At least we would have a common solution to the criminalisation phenomenon with the global abolition of the objective test in criminal negligence. Then the sovereign rights of port states and flag states could remain intact and their respective judicial systems respected. But that ain't going to happen!

In the situation of the current law, which can be guessed to perpetuate due to the priority of the normative ethics of society, the essential leveller, the ultimate consequence of the passage of a just trial is how the punishment will fit the crime.

Some invaluable guidance has been given by the European Union in this context, which was severely tested by a case that was heard by the European Court of Justice in October 2007 and affirms good precedent for the concept. The decision in the case of the *Commission of the European Communities v Council of the European Union*[2] focused heavily on a constitutional conflict within the Union addressing the safety of maritime transport, but clarified principles that, applied more widely, are crucial to this project.

The philosophy in the Treaty of Amsterdam for judicial co-operation in criminal matters[3] specifies, perhaps somewhat narrowly for the tastes of some, that the Union's objective is to provide its citizens with a high level of safety within an area of freedom, security and justice by developing common action among the member states in the fields of police and judicial co-operation in criminal matters, while defining the objective more closely to prevent and combat crime, organised or otherwise, in particular terrorism, trafficking in persons and offences against children, illicit drug trafficking and illicit arms trafficking, corruption and fraud.

Nothing there about maritime safety, and nothing on the Union's power to make new criminal law.

Central to the argument in this case was the court's observation in the judgment that the common transport policy is one of the foundations of the European Union, with its primary objective to improve maritime safety and protect the marine environment. The decision supported the finding in the previous case of the *Commission v The Council*[4] that although the general principle subsists that it is not for the European Community to legislate new criminal law or make rules of criminal procedure, which fall solidly within the jurisdiction of each member

---

2 Case C-440/05 *Commission v Council*.
3 See Title VI of the Treaty.
4 Case C-176/03.

state, nevertheless in the situation in which measures have to be put in place to deter the commission of serious environmental offences, those measures must have the common purpose of implementing effective, proportionate and dissuasive criminal penalties within individual jurisdictions, and to this extent the law-making process within the European Union legislature has the right under the Treaty of Amsterdam to require member states to implement such penalties in order to ensure that the rules that it lays down in the field of environmental protection are fully effective. But the logic of the argument goes beyond this, for the philosophy of the European Union demands a harmonised process that establishes a level playing field across Europe; thus criminal punishment in one state must be consistent with that in another.

The court's decision exposed the supreme difficulty, however, in that the Community has the power to compel member states to provide those criminal penalties, but has no power to tell the member states how to do it. In other words, the power to determine the type and level of penalties to be applied remains within the sovereign jurisdiction of the member state concerned, and on this occasion the European Union has no right to trespass on those rights that are so jealously guarded within the understanding of the word 'sovereignty'.

This concept of international law can be transposed to the issue in context, to reveal the consequence that, while UNCLOS compels port states and flag states to implement regimes of criminal law for the protection of the marine environment, it leaves the determination and technicality of the punishment to the individual systems of the states concerned.

In the case of the criminalisation of the senior manager, be they master, or pilot in command, or air traffic controller, this presents an ultimate hurdle to a solution, for such sovereign rights must be respected. The solution, however, is revealed by logical extension of the argument in the ECJ decision: whoever shall have jurisdiction matters not; it is the determination of the type and level of penalty that is relevant to the master; namely, the process of sentencing. And that can be harmonised very simply by the ratification of sentencing guidelines across the community of port and flag states.

In this context a solution can be explored that has some precedent in the English legal system, which, after all, enjoys the confidence of the maritime world; indeed, London remains supreme as the centre for dispute resolution thanks to the faith that is placed in English admiralty law. The precedent can be identified in the work of the Sentencing Advisory Panel and the Sentencing Guidelines Council, which have established roles in the UK to encourage and develop consistency in sentencing in UK courts. The key feature of their work has involved the promulgation of guidelines in order to aid courts in the complex decision-making process involved in sentencing. In the sphere of this project, sentencing should be uniform, just as the accountability under international law is uniform.

8.2 The foundation of sentencing: Culpability and harm

The inescapable constant in sentencing practice is that it is a slave to the norma-tive ethics of society. While the strict liability offences provided in UNCLOS and MARPOL clearly are intended to deliver redress, it is axiomatic that the redress in question is a matter for resolution between the state parties to the convention concerned. How the normative ethics of the society in whose juris-diction the issue will be tried will demand retribution is an entirely separate matter, which has already been acutely observed, not least in the case of the *Hebei Spirit.*

Seeking to punish the senior manager as the most convenient person to blame for a corporate crime is, therefore, the prime function for the guidelines to avoid. Upon this foundation, the principles of appropriate sentencing can be built.

As representative of the flag state, the errant master has behaved in such a way that the flag state's convention obligations to the port state have been broken. If the port state is to have jurisdiction in the prosecution of the master, therefore, it must establish the culpability of the master in the breach of the port state's sovereign laws, which have been implemented, in theory at least, by virtue of its convention rights and obligations with the flag state.

The Sentencing Guidelines Council published a helpful paper in 2004[5] which was updated in 2015, addressing overarching and general principles relating to the sentencing of offenders. Perhaps the most important change in sentencing guidance, was that which reviewed the range of fines: £180,000 to £20 million.

The Council has always placed great faith in the wisdom of the Criminal Justice Act 2003, which broadly compels the court to take into account five purposes of sentencing when dealing with convicted offenders: the punishment of offenders, the reduction of crime (including its reduction by deterrence), the reform and rehabilitation of offenders, the protection of the public, and the making of reparation by offenders to persons affected by their offence.[6] The application of those purposes in the context of this work in fact underpins the relevance of all save the reform of offenders, which is not a matter with which the port state is likely to concern itself.

The overarching obligation on the court is to pass a sentence that is fair and proportionate when considered with the seriousness of the offence. The serious-ness of an offence is determined by two main parameters: the culpability of the offender and the harm caused or risked being caused by the offence. Consequently,

---

5 Anon, current ed 2015, *Overarching Principle: Seriousness*, Sentencing Guidelines Secretariat, London. Effective from 1 February 2016. See www.sentencingcouncil.org.uk/wp-content/uploads/HS-offences-definitive-guideline-FINAL-web.pdf.
6 Section 142(1) of the Criminal Justice Act 2003.

in the sentencing process following conviction, Step One requires the judge to determine the seriousness of the offence. The Guidelines rather emphasise the obvious that '*By definition, the harm and culpability involved in corporate manslaughter will be very serious. Every case will involve death and corporate fault at a high level.*'

It will be borne in mind that the jury has already returned a verdict of guilty by the time the judge assesses the factors set out in the guidance, which obliges them to ask:

(a) *How foreseeable was serious injury?*

This raises, once again, the issue as to whether the foreseeability should be subjective or objective – in criminal proceedings it should be the foreseeability in the eyes of the master at the time they have to make their fateful decisions, whereas foreseeability is an objective issue subject to tests in the tort of negligence at common law.

Some guidance is given to the judge, who might consider failure to heed warnings or advice from the authorities, employees or others or to respond appropriately to 'near misses' arising in similar circumstances. If this were the case, the repeated concerns of masters regarding safety procedures and commercial pressure in the case of the *Herald* sisters might be relevant factors.

(b) *How far short of the appropriate standard did the offender fall?*

In this case the judge must harness the senior manager's failure to meet the standard reasonably to be expected of them, to the company's culpability in allowing the standard to have been set so far below the minimum that was expected, for which the evidence has so frequently been relied on in breaches of health and safety regulations.

(c) *How common is this kind of breach in this organisation?*

The management failure at a senior level is considered against the wider practice in the organisation, which must have been discovered in the trial process. The guidance suggests two questions that the judge may consider in this context:

•   How widespread was the non-compliance?
•   Was it isolated in extent or, for example, indicative of a systematic departure from good practice across the offender's operations or representative of systemic failings?

(d) Was there more than one death, or a high risk of further deaths, or serious personal injury in addition to death?

The Council views this as indicative of culpability in corporate manslaughter cases. While the general principles of criminal law are offended by the admissibility of evidence of other crimes in determining liability, in sentencing the offender the seriousness of the case may be reflected in the number of deaths, very serious personal injuries or people put at high risk of death.

Culpability, or blameworthiness on the part of the offender, will be determined by such factors as motivation, whether the offence was planned or spontaneous or whether the offender was in a position of trust – or responsibility. Such features manifestly lend themselves to considering the position of the master in a casualty event and, thus, the relevance to the task in context is compelling. Culpability has been analysed to have four levels, which determine the seriousness attached to the mens rea of the offender[7] and can be paraphrased to apply specifically in this case as follows:

1   The master had the intention to cause harm, with the highest culpability when the offence itself was planned. The worse the harm intended, the greater the seriousness.
2   The management failure resulted because the master was reckless as to whether harm would be caused, that is, where the master appreciated that at least some harm would be caused but proceeded anyway, giving no thought to the consequences even though the extent of the risk would be obvious to most masters in that position.
3   The master, as senior manager, had knowledge of the specific risks entailed by their actions even though they did not intend to cause the harm that resulted.
4   The master was guilty of negligence and the company must be tainted with that in its overall management failure.

On the face of it, the last level arouses suspicions that this position is unsafe, in that it perpetuates the mischief of criminal negligence. The Council would argue a relevant point, though, in that strict liability offences, in which culpability need not be proved for the purpose of obtaining a conviction, will still require the consideration of culpability in deciding sentence. When transposed to the wider concept of blameworthiness generally, this raises the fascinating argument that the objective test that is central to the defective concept of criminal negligence could yet play a role in sentencing.

In *R v F Howe & Son*,[8] a case involving breach of health and safety law, the Court of Appeal gave a non-exhaustive list of particular aggravating and mitigating factors that might be relevant when deciding sentence. A deliberate failure by the offender to heed warnings would amount to an aggravating factor; as would a deliberate breach with a view to profit or a risk run specifically in order to save money. By contrast, steps taken to remedy the deficiencies after they were drawn to the offender's attention would amount to a mitigating factor. In fairness, however, such matters have probative value in determining the

---

7   *Overarching Principle: Seriousness*, Sentencing Guidelines Secretariat, p4.
8   *R v F Howe & Son (Engineers) Ltd* [1999] 2 All ER 249.

offender's 'inner posture', that state of mind that embraces consciousness and acceptance of the risk, even if it were not the primary consequence desired by the offender. The test for the 'inner posture' must necessarily be subjective, though, which renders an evaluation by the standard of negligence unsafe, yet again. This conclusion is underpinned by the guidance of the Health and Safety Executive,[9] which identifies a factor to be considered in sentencing that may indicate a higher element of culpability, if the offender deliberately or recklessly violated the law, as opposed to breaching it as a result of carelessness, thus confirming the validity of the approach of determining the offender's state of mind. In conclusion, it is apparent that the same issues of the mental element apply in establishing liability as in sentencing and so level 4 in the Council's advice must be discredited.

Harm must always be judged in the light of, and, therefore, must follow the determination of, culpability. The Council has analysed the parameter of harm to cover three types:·

1   Harm to the individual, who may suffer death, personal injury, psychological stress or financial loss; in other words, issues that are personal to the victim in question, and cause a particular impact that the court should reasonably take into account when determining the seriousness of the offence.
2   Harm to the community, which widens the impact from the individual considered above to the well-being or otherwise of the local society, or society at large.
3   Other types of harm, which the Council had difficulty in characterising but, in the context of a pollution casualty, may describe the effect on wildlife and the marine environment; but there may be human victims as well who suffer financially or psychologically as a result of the environmental damage or the suffering inflicted upon animals as a result of the casualty that gave rise to the offence.

The Council embraced the notion that some conduct is criminalised purely by the normative ethics of society, in particular when public feeling is inflamed by the consequences of the behaviour, which *can influence public perception of the harm caused*.[10] The Council promptly dismissed this highly pertinent factor in 49 words, but the issue is emphasised, nevertheless, leading to the conclusion that sentencing has a natural affinity with the normative ethics of society, which may not be justified within the concept of jurisprudence, as this work has identified exhaustively. Mr Adomako may or may not have been negligent in the concept

9   New Guidelines have come into effect as of 1 February 2016. See https://www.sentencingcouncil. org.uk/wp-content/uploads/HS-offences-definitive-guideline-FINAL-web1.pdf.
10 *Overarching Principle: Seriousness*, Sentencing Guidelines Secretariat, p5.

of civil law, but the concept was translated to the criminal scenario in order to meet the public demand for a criminal consequence for the harm caused. In these terms, the master and crew of the *Sewol* endured the same fate when the state prosecutor secured a conviction on the criminal damage charge, which entitled the court to impose prison sentences.

8.3 The quantum

Having addressed the aggravating factors of culpability and harm, the 2015 Sentencing Guidelines addresses the next step in the quantum of the fine, within the range of £180,000 to £20 million. In this context, the Council never intended to be laconic, and succeeded beyond its wildest dreams. It did its best to achieve clarity, though, with relevant tables that lead the judge to focus on the organisation's annual turnover to reach a starting point, and then consider further adjustment within the category range for aggravating and mitigating features. The judge may then refer to other financial factors in order to ensure that the proposed fine is proportionate.

These steps can only be made to work if the company provides comprehensive accounts for the last three years, to enable the court to make an accurate assessment of its financial status. In the absence of such disclosure, or where the court is not satisfied that it has been given sufficient reliable information, the judge will be entitled to draw reasonable inferences as to the company's real balance sheet from evidence that they have heard and from all the circumstances of the case, which may include the inference that the offender can pay any fine.

Having reached a decision on the fine to be imposed, the guidance then advises the judge to '*step back, review and, if necessary, adjust the initial fine based on turnover to ensure that it fulfils the objectives of sentencing for these offences. The court may adjust the fine upwards or downwards, including outside the range.*'

The Council was alive to the economic realities of business in advising the sentencing judge to '*examine the financial circumstances of the offender in the round to assess the economic realities of the organisation and the most efficacious way of giving effect to the purposes of sentencing*'. In finalising the sentence, the court should have regard to the following factors:

- The profitability of an organisation will be relevant in so far as an organisation that makes only a small profit relative to its turnover may deserve a downward adjustment of the fine, or vice versa.
- In much the same way as courts in the United States determine the quantum of punitive damages, a quantifiable economic advantage derived from the offence should normally be added to the fine.[11]

---

11 See *Grimshaw v Ford*, supra.

- Whether the fine will have the effect of putting the offender out of business will be relevant. The guidance states that '*in some cases this may be an acceptable consequence*', which perpetuates the validity of the comments of Judge Boney in sentencing Mobile Sweepers (Reading) Limited.[12]

The Council has also perpetuated the wisdom of taking into account the power company's ability to pay the full quantum, allowing time for payment or ordering that the amount be paid in instalments, if necessary over a number of years.

Other factors will also be relevant in sentencing, such as wider impacts of the fine within the organisation, such as the impact that the fine would have on the company's ability to pay for the improvement of conditions that would extinguish or reduce the risk of a similar fatal accident again; but the judge emphatically should not consider any mitigating factor in the financial impact that the fine may have on shareholders or directors.

So far we have not addressed two significant factors in sentencing, which are addressed in the Guidelines:

1   Reduction for guilty pleas
     The court should take account of any potential reduction for a guilty plea in accordance with section 144 of the Criminal Justice Act 2003 and the guilty plea guideline.
2   Remediation
     It is notoriously difficult to address the court on mitigation after a jury has returned a verdict of guilty in a trial. But one issue arises out of section 9 of the 2007 Act, and puts the company in a better light, namely if, at the time of sentencing, it has complied with a prosecution notice to remedy any specific failings involved in the offence. Compliance with the notice should be rewarded in a reduced fine. The cost to which the company is put in complying with the order, which requires only what should already have been done, should not ordinarily be taken into account in fixing the fine.

The wider corporate risk arising out of damaged publicity is a factor that will be readily appreciated in the consequences of a corporate manslaughter case, and the Sentencing Guidelines make full use of this as a deterrent or punishment, in making a feature of publicity orders, addressed by section 10 of the 2007 Act.

It states that a publicity order should ordinarily be imposed in a case of corporate manslaughter, which means that there must be some compelling mitigating reason for not ordering one. It may require publication in a specified manner

---

12 See Chapter 6, supra.

of the fact of the conviction; specified particulars of the offence; the amount of any fine and the terms of any remedial order.

A publicity order is specifically designed to be part of the punishment of the company. As a result, any additional cost of compliance should be considered in fixing the fine. It is not, however, necessary to fix the fine first and then deduct the cost of compliance.

In concluding, it should be added for the sake of completeness that the sentencing judge must give reasons for, and explain the effect of, the sentence, in accordance with section 174 of the Criminal Justice Act 2003.

9 Crisis in civil aviation accountability

9.1 The 'just culture' policy

Writing in 2012, Nemsick and Passeri[1] observed a growing trend in criminal investigations in civil aviation since 2000, quoting one source[2] that reported that '*there were only 27 criminal prosecutions stemming from airline or business jet accidents worldwide from 1956 to 1999 (a 43-year period), compared to at least 28 during the period from 2000 to 2009*'. Nemsick noted that it was not just the pilot in command who was the subject of criminal prosecution, however, but also '*airlines, manufacturers . . . management, engineers, and designers. . . . air traffic controllers, regulatory officials, and maintenance providers*'.

The objective of the Eurocontrol model policy ('the policy') is to provide guidance to enforcement and prosecuting authorities on the criminal investigation and prosecution of potential criminal offences resulting from civil aviation accidents or reported incidents.

A number of civil aviation, air traffic control and prosecuting authorities have endorsed the policy, which provides that no prosecution will be brought against individuals for actions, omissions or decisions that reflect the conduct of a reasonable person under the same circumstances, even when those actions, omissions or decisions may have led to an unpremeditated or inadvertent infringement of the law – but that sovereign jurisdiction will remain unaffected in respect of the prosecution of cases involving allegations of intentional wrongdoing or gross negligence. It is the final clause that gives cause for concern because of developments in the law that have outpaced the evolution of the policy; the key focus is on the growth of criminalisation arising out of the use of gross negligence in prosecuting defendants, convicting professionals for actions that hitherto had

---

1 Nemsick, J and S Passeri, 2012, 'Criminalizing Aviation: Placing Blame Before Safety', accessed via http://apps.americanbar.org/litigation/committees/masstorts/articles/winter2012-criminalizing-aviation-blame-safety.html.
2 Mateou, A and S Michaelides-Mateou, 2010, 'Flying in the Face of Criminalization: The Safety Implications of Prosecuting Aviation Professionals for Accidents', accessed via www.ashgate.com/isbn/9781409407676.

not been regarded by society as crimes at all and that, necessarily, forms the mischief that the policy was intended to abate, and Article 2 of the new European Regulation does nothing to help.[3]

Some qualification of criminal, or gross, negligence is offered in the 'just culture' policy, which provides:[4]

> *there does not seem to be a commonly agreed definition of gross negligence in Europe. It seems to be however generally agreed that gross negligence implies a degree of severity, serious disregard to an obvious risk and profound failure to take such care that is evidently required in the circumstances.*

9.2 The threat: Safety or a demand for accountability?

Save for offences of strict liability, which, by international convention, carry non-criminal financial penalties, we have seen how the prosecution must establish both elements of the crime in question, namely the actus reus, containing all the elements in the definition of the crime except the defendant's mental element, and the mens rea, the defendant's guilty mind in terms of intent or recklessness. The gulf between civil liability and criminal liability rests, ultimately, therefore, on how the law determines blameworthiness. If the differences between the two are irreconcilable, then the gulf must be unbridgeable, which essentially defines the philosophy giving rise to the 'just culture' policy. But state law-makers and prosecutors are not listening because this manifestly fails to meet the demands placed on them to establish criminal accountability in circumstances in which there would be nobody else to blame.

This is where the Corporate Manslaughter and Corporate Homicide Act 2007 comes in and, serendipitously, draws in the issue of corporate accountability that defines another facet of the policy. It is quite possible that the UK Parliament intended to bridge the gulf with a cunning plan to simplify convictions of gross negligence manslaughter against companies. The offence is described in section 1, by which a company is guilty of an offence if the way in which its activities are managed or organised causes a person's death, and amounts to a gross breach of a relevant duty of care owed by the company. But the company is guilty of an offence only if the way in which its activities are managed or organised by its senior management is a substantial element of that breach. For the purposes of this Act, a 'relevant duty of care' means any of the duties owed by it 'under the law of negligence' according to civil law. It is noteworthy that

---

3 Regulation (EU) No 376/2014 of the European Parliament and of the Council merely parroting the definition of 'just culture'.
4 Anon, 2012,'Just Culture Policy, European Organisation for the Safety of Air Navigation (ERURON-TROL)', www.eurocontrol.int.

this does not offer any distinction from gross negligence because, in English civil law, there is no distinction. In the 2007 case of *Tradigrain v Internek*[5] the Court of Appeal had to consider this very problem by the applied principle in German law, which requires the satisfaction of two elements:

- an objective element involving a failure to exercise ordinary care where there is a clear risk of harm;
- a subjective element in the form of an absence of anything that renders the act or omission excusable.

Article 33 of the American Criminal Code[6] possibly offers clearer guidance, providing that an act committed with express intent to bring the desired consequence upon the victim – or with the acknowledgment of the *inevitability* of such a consequence by the defendant's action – shall be considered as a crime, and can be paraphrased as follows:

1   A crime will be committed negligently if the defendant foresaw the consequence of their action as reckless, that is, if the defendant saw the risk or inevitability of the consequence in the action, and went ahead with the action nevertheless, thus allowing the consequence to follow or treating the risk with indifference.
2   By comparison, a crime will be committed by negligence if the defendant either had foreseen the possibility of the risk to the victim and expected without valid reasons that the consequence would be prevented, or had not foreseen the possibility of the consequence but should have done.

A great deal of disagreement, not to say confusion, bedevils the analysis of the two as discrete levels of negligence, both in academic arguments and in case law, giving rise to the inevitability of uncertainty in the criminal process. The constant factor running through all of them, clearly, touches upon the defendant's state of mind, which must be established by a subjective test. It will be recalled that in *R v G*[7] Lord Bingham articulated the point beyond any doubt that conviction of a serious crime should depend on proof not simply that the defendant caused (by act or omission) an injurious result to another but that his state of mind when so acting was culpable. Taking an obvious and significant risk by intention or recklessness would satisfy Lord Bingham of a guilty mind but not if the defendant did not perceive the risk; whatever that made him, it did not

---

5   *Tradigrain SA v Internek* [2007] EWCA Civ 154.
6   Criminal Negligence, Article 33.1.
7   *R v G* [2004] 1 AC 1034.

make him a criminal.[8] And it cannot be unravelled from the reason why Judge
Bender so forcefully ruled a consideration of a mere error of judgment out of
the test for negligence in the US case of *Passarello v Grumbine*:[9] the objective test
is the only thing that will do in negligence. To seek to translate this test from
the civil to the criminal context renders its character unsuitable to the task – in
which case criminal negligence must be fatally flawed; but the criminalisation
phenomenon continues apace. The weakness in the 'just culture' policy appears
to grow from the fact that its objective, defined at the top of this chapter, has
not moved forward to meet the challenge of criminal negligence, which has
moved forward by the hand of the same prosecuting authorities. The practical effect has been discussed with pinpoint accuracy by Bert Ruitenberg in his
paper 'Court case against Dutch Air Traffic Controllers',[10] which concerned
the criminal prosecution of three Dutch air traffic controllers following an
incident at Amsterdam Schiphol airport on 10 December 1998 between a Delta
Air Lines Boeing 767 and a towed Boeing 747. The asymmetric development
between the policy and state prosecutions has led to Ruitenberg's conclusion
that Dutch air traffic controllers:

> *will have to do their work with in the back of their minds the bewildering knowledge
> that if anything they do or don't do is perceived as possibly dangerous by the legal
> authorities, they may face criminal prosecution. The highest level of public prosecutors
> in The Netherlands have admittedly stated that they will only prosecute in 'serious
> cases' but they have not provided an explanation of what exactly the word 'serious'
> means in this respect, which doesn't help to make it easier for the controllers. A lot
> of work remains to be done.*[11]

The other critical feature of the policy that demands review concerns the policy
statement that:

> *An incident report filed under a mandatory and voluntary occurrence reporting
> scheme cannot be used as evidence in criminal proceedings against the reporter. Acci-
> dents and incident reports done by investigating bodies or entities under ICAO
> Annex 13 and EU Regulation No 996/2010 cannot be used in criminal proceed-
> ings against individuals.*

---

8 *'Such a person may fairly be accused of stupidity or lack of imagination, but neither of those failings should expose
   him to conviction of serious crime or the risk of punishment.'*
9 *Steven P Passarello and Others v Rowena T Grumbine and Others*, No 1399 WDA 2010; 2011 PA Super
   199.
10 Ruitenberg, B, 2002, *Court case against Dutch Air Traffic Controllers*, LNVL, Amsterdam.
11 Ibid, p5.

That being said, a memorandum of understanding[12] between the Crown Prosecution Service (CPS) and the UK Accident Investigation Branches (AIBs) contains basic principles of co-operation, in that all evidence and factual information (except where there are specific legislative bars), but not opinions or analysis, can be disclosed between the AIBs and the CPS; but what is emphasised is that, even so, the ability of witnesses to be able to talk openly to an accident investigator is fundamental to the operation of the AIBs.

We have seen the relevance of the 2014 decision in *Hoyle v Rogers*[13] when considering the use of a statutory report in corporate manslaughter proceedings, but the case presents a deeper threat still in the just culture concept because, when the Court of Appeal upheld the lower court's decision to allow the AAIB report in evidence in proceedings, the consequences give rise to three particular issues:

1   In accordance with normal rules of evidence, the maker of a report ordered to be admitted under UK law in Part 32 of the Civil Procedure Rules must be available for cross-examination; otherwise the robustness of assertions of fact or opinion contained in the report would be undermined as unsafe. The effect is that the confidentiality of the investigators contributing to the report may be more cautious about the statements they make, diluting their contribution to air safety.

2   As we have seen above, such opinions that could lead to a court's finding of negligence in civil proceedings may subsequently underpin a decision to arraign a defendant on charges of criminal negligence.

3   The downstream consequence is that interviewees in the investigation process may be reluctant to co-operate with the investigating authorities and, despite state regulations compelling their co-operation, would be justified by their privilege against self-incrimination, entitling them to be cautioned before an interview and to have independent legal advice throughout the interview, so that they may have counsel on their right to silence. The further dilution of the value of such investigations to air safety is obvious.

European Regulation No 376/2014 has been vaunted as a guardian of the rights of individuals against such abuse but, even at such a delicate stage in its nascent development, its value in this context must be cast in doubt. Article 15.2 provides that information derived from occurrence reports shall be used only for the purpose for which it has been collected and that member states '*shall not make available or use the information on occurrences in order to attribute blame or*

---

12 https://www.cps.gov.uk/legal/assets/uploads/files/MOU%20between%20CPA%20and%20AIBs%20revised%20version%2030.10.08.pdf.

13 *Scott Hoyle v Julia Mary Rogers and Nicola Lucinda Rogers and Secretary of State for Transport (1st Intervener) and International Air Transport Association (2nd Intervener)* [2014] 3 WLR 148, [2014] CP Rep 30, [2014] EWCA Civ 257, [2014] 3 All ER 550.

liability. . . . or for any purpose other than the maintenance or improvement of aviation safety'. The case of *Hoyle v Rogers* puts such a noble provision firmly in its place. Most pertinently, Article 16 provides in paragraph 10 that the protection afforded to individuals shall not apply,

> *in cases of wilful misconduct or where there has been a manifest, severe and serious disregard of an obvious risk and profound failure of professional responsibility to take such care as is evidently required in the circumstances, causing foreseeable damage to a person or property, or which seriously compromises the level of aviation safety.*

This does nothing more than underline the principle that a state's criminal law shall remain inalienable within its sovereign jurisdiction. There can be no qualification of this, so the mischief of criminal negligence and its uncertain application between different regimes remains unaltered. However unjust it may seem to the rest of the world, the rest of the world cannot do anything about it, thus validating the criminalisation phenomenon even if it is inconsistent with the body of international understanding as perceived in 'just culture'. This concept has received the unimpeachable authority of the European Court of Human Rights, which held in a marine case alleging criminal negligence:

> *The Court. . . . noted in that connection the States' powers and obligations regarding the prevention of marine pollution and the unanimous determination among States and European and international organisations to identify those responsible, to ensure that they appeared to stand trial and to punish them.*[14]

It is inevitable that any discussion or analysis of 'just culture' that ignores the gorilla sitting in the corner, called gross negligence, will merely perpetuate the problem of criminalisation, which, ultimately, would defeat the whole purpose of the policy to protect responsible professionals who are trying to do their job.

9.3 The *Schiphol Air Traffic Controllers* case

The prosecution of the three Dutch air traffic controllers in the Amsterdam incident in 1998 provides an excellent case study in this context. A great deal of highly competent analysis has been published, none more so than that of Bert Ruitenberg in 2002,[15] and it is not intended here to address the key features for any purpose other than as a summary.

---

14 *Mangouras v Spain* (12050/04); para 3 Summary of Judgment.
15 Ruitenberg, B, 2002, *Court case against Dutch air traffic controllers*, International Federation of Air Traffic Controllers' Associations, accessed via International Federation of Air Traffic Controllers' Associations.

On 10 December 1998, an incident occurred at Schiphol (Amsterdam) Airport in which a Delta Air Lines Boeing 767 aborted its take-off roll when the pilots observed a towed Boeing 747 crossing the runway in front of them. At the time of the incident, low visibility procedures were in force. After unclear radio transmissions with the tow truck driver, an assistant controller had passed her interpretation of the tow's position to the trainee controller responsible for the runway. The assistant controller did not have a screen that could show ground radar pictures. The trainee controller did, and took the position of the tow at the edge of the runway to mean that the crossing had been completed. Buttons on a newly added panel in the tower for controlling lighted stop-bars at runway intersections proved ambiguous, but at the time all looked in order, and he cleared the other jet for take-off. Meanwhile, the coach of the trainee controller was performing supervisor duties in the tower.

Air accident investigations were carried out by the Incident Investigation Department of ATC The Netherlands (LVNL),[16] and the Dutch Transport Safety Board (DTSB).[17] It is emphasised that such reports were carried out for the purpose of air safety, not for the prosecution of an offender. Both investigations arrived at similar conclusions. Contributing factors identified in the LVNL report included the following items:

- There was uncertainty about the operation of buttons on a newly added panel in the tower for the control of stop-bars at the runway intersection where the tow was crossing. In addition, the labelling of these buttons was found to be ambiguous.
- The working position of the assistant controller was not equipped with a screen on which a ground radar picture could be selected.
- The coach of the trainee controller simultaneously had to perform supervisor duties in the tower.
- LVNL issued 23 recommendations, all of them aimed at rectifying systemic arrangements in, for example, design, layout, staffing, coaching, communication and handovers.

The DTSB report identified the following causal factors:

- low visibility weather conditions that prevented air traffic control to visually identify vehicles on the ground;
- inadequate information during the radio communications between the tow-combination and tower;
- misinterpretation of position and movement of the tow;

16 Report published 4 March 1999.
17 Report published January 2001.

- take-off clearance without positive confirmation that the runway was unobstructed;
- insufficient teamwork and supervision.

Both reports made recommendations that were all aimed at correcting identified systemic deficiencies in the organisation of air traffic control generally and Schiphol in particular. But, two years after the incident, the Dutch aviation prosecutor went much further, by identifying grounds to establish criminal liability for gross negligence, although no fatal consequences had followed. All were in the air traffic control service, were on duty at the time of the incident, consisting of the trainee, the coach/supervisor and the assistant controller. They were all charged with *'the provision of air traffic control in a dangerous manner, or in a manner that could be dangerous, to persons or properties'*.

At the first hearing, held in August 2001, the judge ruled that the assistant controller was not guilty, but that both the trainee and the coach/supervisor were. They were sentenced to a fine or 20 days' imprisonment. The trainee and the coach/supervisor lodged an appeal, while the prosecutor, equally disappointed, appealed against the assistant controller's acquittal. In September 2002 nearly four years after the incident – the appeal was heard, in which the court found all three accused guilty as charged but did not impose any sentence. This determination treated the case as an *'infringement of the law'* rather than an *'offence against the law'*, a somewhat difficult decision to rationalise because it meant, essentially, that they had not been guilty of a criminal offence but were culpable, in that they were to blame, nevertheless, as one would imagine culpability in a case of strict liability, when the probative value of any evidence is not tested. Indeed, the only admissible defence against such a determination would have been if the defendant was off duty and not at their work station at all. Remarkably, the determination also had the effect of removing any option of appeal because there was no conviction of an offence and no punishment.

Noting how unsafe the applicable law was in this case, Ruitenberg added that:

> Even before the ruling of this court ATC The Netherlands to its credit had made attempts to change the text of the relevant article in Dutch Law, to include qualifications such as 'deliberate act', 'gross negligence', 'wilful misconduct' et cetera.

While Ruitenberg's opinion goes to the heart of 'just culture', the prosecuting authorities in states around the world have moved on with their own agendas. The downstream consequence is a move away from the concept of the just culture, and its replacement with something that many would call a blame culture, leading to criminal accountability and, consequently, corporate accountability by the employer who is vicariously liable for such behaviour that the jury has found to amount to a management failure.

9.4 The Überlingen disaster

Any study of accountability in the environment in which we must apportion responsibility between pilots and air traffic controllers must involve a discussion of the Überlingen mid-air collision.

Late at night on 1 July 2002, Bashkirian Airlines Flight 2937, flown by a Russian Tupolev Tu–154M passenger jet carrying 60 passengers, including 45 school children, and nine crew, and DHL Flight 611, a Boeing 757–23APF cargo jet manned by two pilots, were flying at flight level 360 (that is, 36,000 feet, or 10,973 metres) on a collision course. Despite being just inside the German border, the airspace was controlled from Zürich, Switzerland, by the private Swiss airspace control company Skyguide.

Only one air traffic controller, Peter Nielsen of ACC Zurich, was controlling the airspace through which the aircraft were flying. The other controller on duty was resting in another room, which was against the regulations, but had been a common practice for years and, critically for us, this was known and tolerated by management. The ground-based optical collision warning system, which would have alerted the controller to imminent collisions early, had been switched off for maintenance, but Nielsen was unaware of this. There still was an audible warning system, which released a warning, but it was not heard by anyone present at that time, although no error in this system could be found in a subsequent technical audit, and even if Nielsen had heard this warning, at that time finding a useful resolution order by the air traffic controller would not have been possible.

Nielsen, working two workstations at the same time, did not realise the emerging danger in time and thus failed to keep the aircraft at a safe distance from each other. As if that were not enough, he was distracted by another aircraft movement involving an Airbus approaching Friedrichshafen, which critically was complicated because he had lost the telecommunications with the airport.

Less than a minute before the accident did he realise the danger and contacted Flight 2937, instructing the pilot to descend by a thousand feet to avoid collision with crossing traffic (Flight 611). Seconds after the Russian crew initiated the descent, however, their TCAS traffic collision avoidance system instructed them to climb, while at about the same time the TCAS on Flight 611 instructed the pilots of that aircraft to descend. Had both aircraft followed those automated instructions, the collision would not have occurred.

Flight 611's pilots on the Boeing followed their TCAS instruction and initiated a descent, but could not immediately inform Nielsen because the controller was dealing with Flight 2937. About eight seconds before the collision, Flight 611's descent rate was about 2,400 feet per minute (12 metres per second), not as rapid as the 2,500 to 3,000 feet per minute (13 to 15 metres per second) range advised by TCAS. Having already commenced his descent, as instructed by the controller, the pilot of the Tupolev disregarded the TCAS instruction to climb, thus both planes were now descending.

Unaware of the TCAS-issued alerts, Nielsen repeated his instruction to Flight 2937 to descend, giving the Tupolev crew incorrect information as to the position of the DHL plane. Maintenance work was being carried out on the main radar system, which meant that the controllers were forced to use a slower system.

The aircraft collided at almost a right angle at an altitude of 34,890 feet, with the Boeing's vertical stabiliser slicing completely through Flight 2937's fuselage just ahead of the Tupolev's wings. The Tupolev exploded and broke into several pieces, scattering wreckage over a wide area. The nose section of the aircraft fell vertically, while the tail section with the engines continued, stalled, and fell. The crippled Boeing struggled for a further seven kilometres (four miles) before crashing into a wooded area close to the village of Taisersdorf at a 70-degree downward angle. Each engine ended up several hundred metres away from the main wreckage, and the tail section was torn from the fuselage by trees just before impact.

All 69 people on the Tupolev, and the two on board the Boeing, died.

On 19 May 2004, the German Federal Bureau of Aircraft Accidents Investigation published its determination[18] that the accident had been caused by shortcomings in the Swiss air traffic control system supervising the flights at the time of the accident and by ambiguities in the use of TCAS, the on-board aircraft collision avoidance system.

While Tadros valiantly warns against the instinct to find some blame for death instead of tracking the wrongfulness of the killing, it is more difficult to steer a jury on that course. After all, from the moment when the jury enters the retiring room, their deliberations are absolutely private and open to no interference, well-meaning as it might be. And juries are notoriously capricious, doubtless because they are nothing more than an arbitrary selection of 12 of the defendant's peers, and they are as open to anger and sentiment as anybody.

Dekker refers to Snook's investigation of a friendly fire incident in the first Iraq war,[19] when the author stated how his original anger at the consequence changed after his research indicated that, in fact, it had not been anybody's fault.

---

18   *Bundesstelle für Flugunfalluntersuchung*, Investigation Report AX001–1–2/02 May 2004. See http://cfapp.icao.int/fsix/sr/reports/02001351_final_report_01.pdf.

19   Snook, S, 2000, *Friendly Fire: the accidental shootdown of US Black hawks over northern Iraq*, Princeton University Press Princeton NJ.

As he put it: '*if nothing was abnormal from a behavioural and organisational perspective – then what?*' Snook was merely analysing the evidence as a jury would. His final, rhetorical question – '*then what?*' – must equate to the element of doubt that should force a jury to return a verdict of not guilty. If you strip away the element of hindsight offered by expert witnesses and others in a case, and what is left simply begs the question '*then what?*', it would be unsafe to put the evidence to the jury and the defendant must be acquitted, just as it has in a number of corporate manslaughter cases that have now been heard under the 2007 Act.

The crisis in the just culture environment is taken further when we come to study the anatomy of a casualty and what we need to take away in lessons to be learned. In their paper reviewing the just culture concept in the light of the mid-Staffordshire medical care case, Dekker and Hugh[20] swiftly cut to the core of the issue by identifying a three-stage process of learning that should follow each casualty:

1   The need to understand what happened
2   The need to prevent it happening again
3   The need to explain suffering in terms of the need for justice.

In terms of corporate manslaughter, at first glance it is only the third element that has relevance; but, in fact, all three are indispensable. Satisfying the demand for justice means not just accounting for the casualty in question but, also, avoiding recurrence. Dekker particularly strikes a chord with the criminal process in corporate manslaughter when he elaborates on the difficulties of establishing the evidence beyond reasonable doubt:

> *particularly when harm has occurred, our assessments of other people's behaviour get coloured by outcome and hindsight biases. Knowledge of outcome affects our evaluation of the quality of decisions, whereas, hindsight increases retrospective estimates of the foreseeability of outcome.*

When applied to the evidence heard in the prosecution of *MNS Mining*, and even more poignantly in the *Tunbridge Wells Hospital* case, it is essential that the jury examines the evidence from the subjective perspective demanded by criminal accountability, rather than by the objective test of the consequences required to establish civil liability in negligence. Once again, the mischief of combining the two into the crime of corporate manslaughter becomes all too clear.

---

20 Dekker, S and T Hugh, 'A just culture after mid-Staffordshire', BMJ August 2014.

10 Lessons to be shared

10.1 Dangers and duties of care: The business of anchor-handling tug supply vessels

On the face of it, many would say that the fatal casualty in a deep sea casualty involving an anchor-handling tug had no synergy with the civil aviation industry that would help them to develop a response to avoid such an accident again. But the *Bourbon Dolphin* case has proved them wrong.

Anchor-handling tugs, often abbreviated to AHTSVs, are extremely powerful deep sea vessels that are designed to handle the dynamic positioning of offshore installations, oil and gas rigs, towing them and anchoring them with massive winches for anchor-handling, while having the capability to transport and deliver supplies from shore to rig, making use of large open decks aft where many operations take place that must be carefully managed according to the ship's safety management system. In many cases, they also maintain a role of an emergency response and rescue vessel, and act as stand-by in case of drifting or towing away threatening objects.

The *Skandi Pacific* is a modern, high-powered anchor-handling vessel designed for field installation operations across a wide range of water depths and environmental conditions. The vessel was just four years old, well bedded-in, well appointed, and well maintained. According to the Australian Transport and Safety Bureau, on 14 July 2015, *Skandi Pacific* was 175 kilometres off the West Australian coast when she had to stop working cargo with the drilling platform *Atwood Osprey* due to heavy weather. The ATSB elaborated only briefly:

> While attempting to shelter from the weather and secure cargo a wave came over the back deck of the vessel and shifted cargo. A crew member was attempting to secure cargo when he was crushed between a moving mini-container and a cargo skip. He was removed to the nearby drill platform to receive medical assistance but died of his injuries.

The ATSB is investigating the casualty,[1] pending which it is not anticipated that sufficient facts or expert conclusions can be drawn upon which to make any opinion, but Paddy Crumlin, the National Secretary of the Maritime Union of Australia, warned of the hazardous life in such operations:

> *The offshore industry is an inherently high safety risk environment, the highest in the country and the world, due to the isolated and unstable nature of seagoing work and the 24/7 requirements placed on seafarers.*

Against this background, let us consider the case of the *Bourbon Dolphin*, and the standard of duty that must be met by the owners and their senior managers.

10.2 The *Bourbon Dolphin* case

At the time of the fatal accident in April 2007, the *Bourbon Dolphin* was just six months old. She was a large, powerful, state-of-the-art anchor-handling vessel, and on the morning of 12 April was the lead tug in a tandem operation moving the Chevron-chartered drilling rig *Transocean Rather*. While shifting the rig's eighth and final anchor, assisting tug *Highland Valour* was unable to maintain its grip on the anchor chain and the resultant tension on *Bourbon Dolphin's* winch, which could safely operate at a maximum of 240 tonnes, soared to at least 330 tonnes and two engines failed. The broadwise burden caused the 2,985-gross-ton tug to capsize, killing eight of the 15 crew. The dead included *Bourbon Dolphin's* master, Oddne Arve Remoy, 44, and his 14-year-old son who was along on sea training, as well as five other Norwegians and one Dane.

As general practice, any anchor-handling operation demands careful risk management, and operational plans must make it top priority for the crew to discontinue if the vessel is exposed to greater tension than the plan allows or if the boat heels enough to get water on the working deck. It is forbidden to connect anchor-towing gear to a winch on one vessel unless that vessel can handle the load alone.

Large as she was, in this case, Bourbon officials apparently stated that *Bourbon Dolphin* was too small to serve as the lead tug on the *Transocean Rather* operation. *Bourbon* Chief Executive Jacques de Chateauvieux said in a technical interview that the tug's master twice asked to stop the operation:

> *Right before the tragedy happened, it was obvious that the conditions were so difficult, mainly because the weight of the chain could not be eased up by vessel Number 2 [Highland Valour]. The captain should have stopped the operation much earlier, even though he was instructed a different way.*

---

1 ATSB Investigation number: 322-MO-2015–005.

A special commission of enquiry[2] that was established, chaired by appellate court judge Inger Lyng, has clarified the course of events and causal factors in connection with the accident. In its report the Commission concluded that it was not possible to show that an individual error, whether technical or human, led to the accident; rather, a series of circumstances acted together to cause the loss of the vessel. The Commission found that the proximate causes of the accident were the vessel's change of course to port so as to get away from a dangerously tense mooring line, at the same time as the inner starboard towing pin was depressed, causing the chain to rest against the outer port towing pin. This gave the chain an altered point and angle of attack on the vessel. Together with the vessel's current load condition, the fact that the roll reduction tank was probably in use, and the effect on the vessel and chain of external forces, caused the vessel to capsize.

The report highlighted a number of indirect factors that contributed to the accident. A combination of weaknesses in the design of the vessel, and failures in the handling of safety systems by the company, by the operator and on the rig, contributed to the various participants on the spot losing control of the operation. Overall, system failures on the part of many of those participants caused a breakdown in safety, so that precautions and protection were lacking, were ignored or were breached, so that the vessel and crew were exposed to a fatal level of risk.

Among the many factors that were defined in the report's findings, we may single out the following as the most important conclusions that would have been relevant to the analysis of liability for criminal negligence:

- Irrespective of the specification of the vessel, the company had no previous experience with the design and ought therefore to have undertaken more critical assessments of the vessel's characteristics, equipment and not least operational limitations, both during her construction and during her subsequent operations under various conditions. The company did not pick up on the fact that the vessel had experienced an unexpected stability-critical incident about two months after delivery.
- In mitigation, the vessel's stability-related challenges were not clearly communicated from shipyard to company and onwards to those who were to operate the vessel.
- Despite ISM's requirement for procedures to be set for the key operations that the vessel was to perform, and despite the fact that anchor-handling was

---

2 For the Norwegian Justice Ministry Report see www.regjeringen.no/en/aktuelt/report-on-the-loss-of-the-bourbon-dolphi/id505100/.

the vessel's main function, there was no vessel-specific anchor-handling procedure in place for her.

- The company did not follow the ISM code's requirement that all risks be
identified.

- The company did not impose sufficient requirements for the crew's quali-
fications for demanding operations. The crew's lack of experience was not
compensated for by the addition of experienced personnel.

- The master was given 1½ hours to familiarise himself with the crew and
vessel and the ongoing operation. In its safety management system the
company has a requirement that new crews should be familiarised with
(inducted into) the vessel before they can take up their duties on board. In
practice the master familiarises himself by overlapping with another master
who knows the vessel, before he himself is given the command.

- Neither the company nor the operator ensured that sufficient time was
made available for hand–over in the crew change.

- The vessel was marketed with continuous bollard pull of 180 tonnes. During an anchor-handling operation, in practice thrusters are always used for
manoeuvring and dynamic positioning. The real bollard pull is then materially reduced. The company did not itself investigate whether the vessel
was suited to the operation, but left this to the master.

- The company did not see to the acquisition of information about the content and scope of the assignment the *Bourbon Dolphin* was set to carry out.
The company did not itself do any review of the Rig Move Procedure
(RMP) with a view to risk exposure for crew and vessel. The company was
thus not in a position to offer guidance.

- The Norwegian classification society Det Norske Veritas (DNV) and the
Norwegian Maritime Directorate were unable to detect the failures in the
company's systems though their audits.

- In specifying the vessel, the operator did not take account of the fact that the
real bollard pull would be materially reduced through use of thrusters. In
practice the *Bourbon Dolphin* was unsuited to dealing with the great forces
to which she was exposed.

- The mooring system and the deployment method chosen were demanding
to handle and vulnerable in relation to environmental forces.

- Planning of the RMP was incomplete. The procedure lacked fundamental
and concrete risk assessments. Weather criteria were not defined and the
forces were calculated for better weather conditions than they chose to
operate in.

- Defined safety barriers were lacking. It was left to the discretion of the rig
and the vessels whether operations should start or be suspended.

- In advance of the operation, no start-up meeting with all involved parties was held. The vessels did not receive sufficient information about what could be expected of them, and the master misunderstood the vessel's role.
- The procedure demanded the use of two vessels that had to operate at close quarters in different phases during the recovery and deployment of anchors.
- The increased risk exposure of the vessels was not reflected in the procedure.
- The procedure lacked provisions for alternative measures (contingency planning), for example in uncontrollable drifting from the run-out line. Nor were there guidelines for when and in what way such alternative measures should be implemented and what if any risk these would involve.
- The deployment of anchor no. 2 was commenced without the considerable drifting during the deployment of the diagonal anchor no. 6 having been evaluated.

Undoubtedly a key feature of the *Bourbon Dolphin* study is not just the facts of the case, but the response taken by the owners, which resulted in a new generation of operational training that supports a self-confident management system that minimises the risk of failure leading to a fatal accident. In a technical interview the company outlined the rationale for the new system:[3]

> *The idea of cockpit management started with the Scandinavian Airlines, and then that was taken up by the marine industry and grew into bridge resource management. Now at Bourbon we are taking it a step further and training for crew resource management.*

10.3 Shared issues in marine and aviation casualties

The United States National Transportation Safety Board has assessed the most common causes of aviation casualties caused by human error. Let us consider some of them against some issues identified in the maritime sector, to gain an understanding of shared problems, from which we can share lessons.

- Lack of communication is highlighted as a major factor by the USNTSB. A report by the Swedish Club published in 2015 suggests that many navigational claims occur due to procedures not being properly followed by crew members, and officers not communicating with each other properly. In addition poor communication between both vessels and bridge team

---

3 See www.professionalmariner.com/March-2010/New-anchor-handling-tug-training-emphasizes-the-view-from-the-aft-deck/.

members and a lack of situational awareness all play a part. Additionally, it will be recalled in the *Pride of Provence* casualty in 2003 that the MAIB concluded inter alia that '*the bridge was manned by a suitable number of qualified and experienced personnel, but they were unable to perform the monitoring tasks allotted to them because they were poorly briefed about the master's intentions*'.[4]

- Loss of situational awareness is another cause identified by the USNTSB. In the *Ovit* casualty, the officer of the watch monitored the vessel's position solely against the intended track. Consequently, his situational awareness was poor. The officer of the watch followed the track shown on the ECDIS display but had such poor situational awareness that it took him 19 minutes to realise the vessel was aground.[5]

- Fatigue. In 2013 the *Danio* ran aground because the chief officer, who was the lone watchkeeper on the bridge, had fallen asleep: '*It is probable that he had fallen asleep during the first hour of his watch and woke only when the vessel grounded. It is very likely that the chief officer was suffering from the cumulative effects of fatigue due to the combination of the 6 hours on / 6 hours off watch routine and frequent disruption to this routine when the vessel was in port.*'[6]

- Lack of teamwork, distraction, lack of assertiveness by the bridge team were all identified as major factors in the casualty report of the *Costa Concordia* casualty. See notably paragraph 5.1 (p. 152ff): '*Bridge team not paying the required attention; Master not relying on the support of the Bridge Team; overall passive attitude of the Bridge Staff.*'[7]

In view of the clear commonality between maritime and aviation casualties, a broader mindset in risk management would allow lessons to be learned from both industries and thus deliver the safety management system demanded by the standards set in the 2007 Act, to co-ordinate recognition of risk, risk assessment, developing strategies to manage it, and mitigation of risk using managerial resources, with the single objective that the law can reasonably demand, to reduce different risks related to a pre-selected domain to the level accepted by society through statutory authority of common law precedents. It is, after all, merely the evidence which demonstrates that a safe management system was in place, and it was conducted by a senior manager within the parameters

4 MAIB, *Report on the investigation of the contact between Pride of Provence and The Southern Breakwater, Dover Harbour, eastern entrance on 18 April 2003.*

5 MAIB, *Report on the investigation of the grounding of Ovit in the Dover Strait on 18 September 2013.*

6 MAIB, *Report on the investigation of the grounding of Danio off Longstone, Farne Islands, England 16 March 2013.*

7 Ministry of Infrastructures and Transports Marine Casualties Investigative Body Cruise Ship Costa Concordia Marine casualty on 13 January 2012 Report on the safety technical investigation.

demanded by Society in its law. No better example can be drawn than that which formed the conclusion of Judge Steel in the *Torepo*:[8]

> *I am quite unable to infer from this that the master was inefficient or incompetent: (i) He had ordered all the appropriate charts at Montevideo. (ii) Initially the vessel shaped for a rendezvous with the pilots. The vessel was equipped with the appropriate charts for that part of the passage (and if necessary a transit via the Cape Horn). (iii) Once the route via the Magellan Straits was confirmed, the second officer prepared a detailed passage plan, which was entered in the register. (iv) The plan was a satisfactory one having regard to the limited material available. (v) The plan could not be completed or implemented without large-scale charts. (vi) The master was informed that pilots would be bringing on board Chilean charts of an appropriately large scale. (vii) Those charts could properly be used for installing the plan as prepared or for review of any plan prepared by the pilots. Faced with difficulties about the supply of charts, the master coped sensibly and properly with passage planning requirements. The decision to transit the Straits was a reasonable decision and not indicative of incompetence on the part of the master. Put shortly, the attack on the master with regard to his attitude to passage planning is no more and no less than a suggestion that he was minded, in the absence of the appropriate large-scale charts, to navigate the Magellan Straits using charts with inappropriate scale. . . . Even on the assumption that the pilot's passage plan was defective in the respects that I have already discussed, I cannot infer that the master was inefficient or incompetent simply by reason of his failure to identify those defects in a very long passage plan for transit through difficult waters. The best advice which the master could and did give was that the progress of the vessel should be monitored along the planned track by parallel indexing. This view was enhanced by the Bridge Procedures Manual . . .*

To summarise, the law demands that the defendant meets the minimum standards of risk management, and in this case the judge was eminently satisfied by the evidence. That is why sharing best practice demonstrates a level of risk management so far in excess of the minimum, that a senior manager can hardly be held to account for an alleged management failure.

For a venture into our last chapter, that will be an absolute necessity.

---

8 *The Torepo* [2002] EWHC 1481 (Admlty).

11 In hazard

The next generation in the High Arctic

11.1 Tensions in the background

Alterations in global climate patterns are warming the Arctic region of North America in a rapid manner and, consequently, melting the polar ice cap. The linear trend in ice extent for December 2013 shows a reduction since 1978 of 3.5 per cent per decade – that is 18,000 square miles per year. While the most notable aspect of 2013 was the much higher September ice extent relative to the record low for 2012, the extent in 2013 was nevertheless low overall.[1]

Paradoxically, this phenomenon presents a new opportunity for deep sea shipping but the same opportunities raise tensions between states that are competing for them. The Northwest Passage is a strategic route from the Atlantic Ocean to the Pacific Ocean through a myriad of islands. Since the European discovery of North America, explorers throughout the world have been fascinated by the possibility of shipping through this region, commercially joining Europe to the Orient. By comparison with the Panama Canal route, the transportation of goods through the Northwest Passage would shorten the voyage from Europe to the Far East by some 5,000 nautical miles.

Issues of sovereignty are at stake, of course; for the state that can establish its rights of ownership under the United Nations Convention on the Law of the Sea (UNCLOS) will be the one that will benefit from the resources. The history of claims and counterclaims over territory in the region predates UNCLOS by nearly a thousand years, though. In recent history, the region held no interest for states and commercial adventurers because the climate rendered any exploitation unviable. It is only with the opportunity for commercial gain that ownership is now being hotly disputed.[2] From Canada's point of view, the time–line starts authoritatively in 1907 when Senator Poirier advocated that Canada's Arctic claim should extend from the mainland of Canada up to the North Pole, bounded by sector lines – the 141st meridian of west longitude to the west and

---

1 Source: National Snow and Ice Data Center http://nsidc.org/arcticseaicenews/.
2 See Sale R and E Potatov, 2010, *The Scramble For The Arctic*, Frances Lincoln, London.

the 60th meridian of west longitude to the east – which would form an apex at the North Pole.[3]

The trouble is that there is no dedicated international treaty for delimiting or regulating the Arctic. Once a state ratifies UNCLOS, it has a limitation period of ten years in order to establish its claim to the continental shelf that is so instrumental in identifying its exclusive economic zone. Of the states that are making claims in the High Arctic, Norway ratified in 1996, Russia in 1997, Canada in 2003, and Denmark in 2007. The other state with a claim, the United States, has not ratified UNCLOS, but has asserted its right to the Northwest Passage as an international waterway between the Atlantic and Pacific Oceans, citing in its support the Corfu Channel case heard by the International Court of Justice in 1949. It has consistently challenged the Canadian right to such sovereignty compromising the Northwest Passage and, in 1985, just to prove its point, Washington sent an icebreaker, *Polar Sea*, through the Northwest Passage without informing Canada or asking permission. In fact, the United States really had to make such a gesture, because of its inherently weak position in not having ratified UNCLOS, which deprived it of the *locus standi* to lodge a formal submission before the United Nations Commission on the Limits of the Continental Shelf under Article 76.

In 2005, a joint project undertaken by the Arctic Council and the International Arctic Science Committee published a 1,042-page report[4] which warned that the reduction in sea ice would have devastating consequences on the wildlife of the region; this would have a downstream consequence on the indigenous peoples who relied upon it as a food resource. But it also emphasised that the same reduction in sea ice would likely increase maritime commerce, both as to ships and access to the resources that those ships would be loading. The obvious consequence presents new employment opportunities for masters, for whom their criminal accountability may be viewed as an occupational hazard. As the commercial opportunities for owners gather pace, the flag state will be anxious to ensure that its obligations under international law are met – and the coastal state will not be taking any chances.

Obligations between states are clearly defined in UNCLOS, Part II section 1 of which provides for the sovereign limits of a coastal state to extend up to 12 nautical miles beyond its land territory and any archipelagic waters; in this area, known as the territorial sea, merchant vessels of all states have the rights of innocent passage; that is, so long as the voyage is not prejudicial to the peace, good order or security of the coastal state. That being said, Article 21 authorises the coastal state to exercise its jurisdiction over such vessels, essentially by statutory

3   McRae, D, 2007, *Arctic Sovereignty? What is at Stake? Behind the Headlines*, Canadian Institute of International Affairs (Canadian International Council), Toronto.
4   ACIA, 2005, *Arctic Climate Impact Assessment – Scientific Report*, Cambridge University Press, Cambridge.

regulations managed by the court process, in order to ensure the state's sovereign rights over matters including, amongst other things, the safety of navigation and the regulation of maritime traffic, the conservation of the living resources of the sea, the prevention of infringement of the fisheries laws and regulations of the coastal state, the preservation of the environment of the coastal state and the prevention, reduction and control of pollution, and the prevention of infringement of the customs, fiscal, immigration or sanitary laws and regulations of the coastal state. Most importantly for the master, Article 21.4 requires that ships of other flag states exercising the right of innocent passage through the territorial sea shall comply with all such laws and regulations and all generally accepted international regulations relating to the prevention of collisions at sea. The key issue to bear in mind, is the focus on the obligation on *ships*, not their *master* – that is, the thing over which the flag state has sovereign management control by reason of the allocation of its flag, in whom they have reposed their confidence in the master who has been clothed with their certificate of competency.

Beyond the territorial sea, the coastal state does not have powers to protect its resources, save those reserved for the exclusive economic zone defined in Part V of the convention, limiting the coastal states' enforcement powers for the purpose of exploring and exploiting, conserving and managing the natural resources, including those in the waters superjacent to the seabed and of the seabed and its subsoil, but limiting the state's jurisdiction, that is, its judicial enforcement, to protect installations and structures (such as drill rigs), the conduct of marine scientific research and a sweeping provision for '*other rights and duties*' defined in the convention.

Of course, the coastal state's jurisdiction can be well established when the calculations of rights from the baseline are agreed by other states. Where there is no such treaty, as in the High Arctic, the master is sailing into potentially disputed waters. And we have not even touched upon the potential flashpoint of disputed boundary rights in international straits. In this case, we are addressing the issue of the Northwest Passage, which Part III of the convention only protects by requiring bordering states to respect by refraining from interrupting the rights of transit passage by a ship of another flag state, save for the protection of safe navigation or the marine environment or resources, or the protection of health and immigration, customs and revenues. The relevance to the Northwest Passage lay in the issues between the United States and Canada; the former demands transit rights through the Passage according to the provisions in UNCLOS for international straits; the latter asserts sovereignty over the Passage which lies, it argues, solidly within the definition of its archipelagic territory.[5]

---

5   Daniels, S, 2012, *The Criminalisation of the Ship's Master. A new approach for the new Millennium*. PhD thesis.

11.2 The race to an Arctic gold rush

Russia claims to have raced to the North Pole first. On 2 August 2007, a Russian maritime polar expedition, *Arktika 2007*, made the first-ever descent to the seabed at the North Pole and planted a Russian flag from a submarine, which also took soil samples to analyse as evidence in support of its claim to the region's mineral resources. A BBC news report[6] dramatically announced that Russia was leading a new 'gold rush' in the High Arctic, but the event should not really have come as a surprise, because as early as December 2001, Russia had laid a formal submission before the United Nations Commission on the Limits of the Continental Shelf under Article 76 of UNCLOS. And the world demand for seabed resources was rising as existing supplies were predicted to dwindle.

UNCLOS has been the key authority underpinning decisions by the International Court of Justice on settling delimitation disputes, which formed the basis upon which the court found unanimously that Honduras had sovereignty over four disputed islands in the Caribbean Sea.[7] In determining the delimitation of the territorial sea, the court confirmed that equidistance remains the yardstick as a general rule – a finding strongly followed in the most recent 2014 judgment in the dispute between Peru and Chile[8] – but that the existence of special circumstances such as geomorphological factors along the relevant coast has a part to play:

> *the equidistance method does not automatically have priority over other methods of delimitation when it comes to fixing an all-purpose boundary covering the territorial sea, the exclusive economic zone, and the continental shelf.*[9]

Russia is depending on it, claiming that the Lomonosov Ridge is an extension of the Russian landmass, which actually reaches beyond the North Pole for Russia's purposes. But that did not stop Canada from expressing a great deal of irritation with the Russian flag-planting gesture, when Peter MacKay, Canada's Foreign Affairs Minister responded:

> *This is posturing. This is the true north strong and free, and they're fooling themselves if they think dropping a flag on the ocean floor is going to change anything. There is no question over Canadian sovereignty in the Arctic. We've made that very clear.*

---

6   BBC News 30 August 2007 by Paul Reynolds, world affairs correspondent, BBC News website.

7   *Case concerning Territorial and Maritime Dispute between Nicaragua and Honduras in the Caribbean Sea (Nicaragua v Honduras),* judgment of 8 October 2007. While the dispute dated back to 1821, at least there was some treaty background, and arbitration proceedings, for the court to work on – in the High Arctic of course there has been no such resolution.

8   *Case concerning Maritime Dispute between Peru and Chile (Peru v Chile)* Judgment of 27 January 2014. This case may be distinguished from the Arctic scenario, however, as it involved the validity and application of a number of international agreements to which Peru and Chile were contracting parties.

9   *Nicaragua v Honduras,* paragraph 272.

We've established — a long time ago — that these are Canadian waters and this is Canadian property. You can't go around the world these days dropping a flag somewhere. This isn't the 14th or 15th century.

Mr MacKay's Russian counterpart, Sergey Lavrov, responded more phlegmatically when questioned at a press conference, reminding the world that Russia had already claimed the submerged ridges forming the territory that would bring the region within its boundaries, and the expedition was merely gathering evidence to support that claim in accordance with a directions order of the UN Commission for further evidence of Russia's claim.[10] Since then, the Russian navy has maintained, and developed, a strategic presence in the Arctic.[11] Its under-sea patrol programme will soon be augmented by the new *Borey* class submarines based on the Barents Sea coast. Equally notable are Russia's power-projection initiatives. In 2012, a large-scale Russian naval exercise was held in the High North that included more than 7,000 personnel and about 20 naval units. During the exercise, the Northern Fleet conducted Russia's first-ever amphibious landing on the Arctic archipelago of the New Siberian Islands.[12]

In the summer of 2013, Moscow held a massive exercise in the Russian far east region – reportedly the biggest 'snap-drill' since the era of the Soviet Union. The exercises involved more than 160,000 servicemen, 1,000 tanks, 130 planes and 70 ships, and came only a month after Russia submitted a claim to the United Nations to extend its 200-mile exclusive economic zone by another 150 miles or 1.2 million square kilometres. Moscow's 'scientific evidence', whose purpose was to corroborate its claim to the seabed being a continuation of the continental shelf, is bitterly contested by other Arctic nations.

Perhaps a more impartial commentary came from the influential monitor Jane's, which stated in December 2013 that President Vladimir Putin and Defence Minister Sergei Shoigu had announced further Arctic militarisation, most importantly the bringing forward of the creation of an Arctic Group of Forces (Army Group) from 2020 to 2014, with plans to form a squadron of ice-breaking warships '*to protect Arctic shipping Routes*'. Infantry forces that are '*to fight in the region*' will also be provided with new equipment. Apparently this move, bringing forward strategic plans by six years, responded to Canada's

10 See Transcript of Remarks and Replies to Media Questions by Russian Minister of Foreign Affairs Sergey Lavrov at Joint Press Conference with Philippine Foreign Affairs Secretary Alberto Romulo, Manila, 3 August 2007, Ministry of Foreign Affairs of the Russian Federation, Moscow.

11 An announcement by Security Council Chief Nikolay Partushev to build new naval bases in the Arctic was reported in August 2012 by Russia Today. See http://rt.com/politics/arctic-ship-marine-base-969/.

12 For further commentary see: http://thediplomat.com/2013/10/the-creeping-militarization-of-the-arctic/.

announcement, six days before, just before a United Nations deadline for registering claims, that it intended to extend its jurisdiction in the polar region.[13]

This should be read in the context of Russia's position not so long ago, when it was unprepared for any confrontation: in September 2010, at a conference on the Arctic held in the Kremlin, President Putin said:

> *Very serious economic and geopolitical interests intersect in the Arctic, but I have no doubt that all the problems existing in the Arctic, including problems over the continental shelf, can be resolved in an atmosphere of partnership.*

But dispute resolution by the International Court of Justice is notoriously slow and, like any judicial decision, the outcome is uncertain and doomed to disappoint at least one (sometimes both) of the parties. In the *Peru v Chile* case, the Republic of Peru commenced proceedings in January 2008; judgment was given six years later, a long time to wait when fishermen are impatiently awaiting a decision on who has the rights to the marine resources.

Back in the High Arctic, with the possibilities presented by global warming, the Canadian government is experiencing new challenges to its claims of sovereignty to territories that it has traditionally regarded as its own, not only in the resource-rich polar regions disputed with Russia, but also in the Northwest Passage, disputed with the United States. Canada's perspective is that they have full sovereignty encompassing the islands and waterways and thereby will assert complete control over all activity in that specific region, in accordance with the general principles defined in UNCLOS, based on the rules concerning determination of baselines in the archipelagic context defined in Part IV. The Canadian government has continually stated that it supports international shipping through the Northwest Passage, as long as Canadian domestic laws, rather than international law, are followed. In July 2007, Prime Minister Stephen Harper reinforced the Canadian position by announcing the construction of up to eight Polar Class 5 Arctic Offshore Patrol Ships and the establishment of a deep-water port in the far north.

There is a further complication in that any coastal state in ice-covered areas has the right under Article 234 of UNCLOS to adopt and enforce non-discriminatory laws and regulations for the prevention, reduction and control of marine pollution from vessels in ice-covered areas within the limits of the exclusive economic zone beyond their territorial jurisdiction, for the safety of navigation and where marine pollution could cause major harm to or irreversible disturbance to the pristine environment of the boreal wilderness. In fact, this Article was adopted as a result of pressure by the Canadian government,

---

13 In May 2016 Janes updated its intelligence with the news that Russia proposed to reinforce the extension of its jurisdiction with an order for two new warships combining the qualities of tug, ice-breaker, and patrol boat. See http://www.janes.com/article/60063/russia-orders-new-project-23550-arctic-corvettes.

which is keenly alive to the fact that, whatever the maritime opportunities for the Northwest Passage, the risks are great: Canada's Arctic archipelago comprises 36,000 islands, islets and rocks, making it one of the most complex marine geographies on Earth.

Naturally, Canada appreciates that environmental interests are not the only ones at stake; Canadian business has real opportunities, as well. In October 2007, Canada's largest ocean-going dry bulk ship operator, Fednav, announced that it was poised to buy a Polar Capesize fleet for anything up to $2 billion, to serve a new iron ore mining development in Canada's High North. The Montreal-based ice-class shipping specialist was reported by Lloyd's List to be investigating yards that could build up to nine Capesize carriers lifting a total of 130,000 deadweight tonnes of high-grade iron ore across the North Atlantic to Europe. While the global recession might have been expected to put a brake on this activity, Fednav simply could not stand back and wait for its competitors to challenge its position. Fednav introduced the *Federal Sable* in 2012, a handysize dry bulk carrier, which will reduce environmental impact while launching a period of growth and renewal for the company, which spread the investment risk in its new fleet with Sumitomo Corporation and Oshima Shipyard.

11.3 Arctic passages – and risk management

Then there was another first in the High Arctic. In September 2013, the two-year-old, Panamanian-flagged bulk carrier *Nordic Orion* arrived in Vancouver to load a cargo of 73,500 tonnes of metallurgical coal for delivery to steelworks in Finland, with a voyage plan originally sailing through the Panama Canal. But a navigable Northwest Passage offered real savings in terms of cost and voyage time, and the ship's Danish owners decided to take the route through the Passage, the first bulk carrier to do so, ever.

It took four days less than it would have taken to traverse the Panama Canal, and its greater depths allowed the *Nordic Orion*, with a deadweight tonnage exceeding 75,000 and a draught of 14 metres, to carry about 25 per cent more coal. The hull and machinery insurers did not reveal the premium for the voyage, but the *Vancouver Globe and Mail* did some homework and guessed that the premium for a ship such as the *Nordic Orion*, nearly new and especially built to cope with ice conditions, would be some $100,000, and that travelling through the Northwest Passage could involve an additional premium of up to 30 per cent. In addition, the *Nordic Orion* sailed with the Canadian coastguard's most capable icebreaker[14] throughout the passage. Even so, sailing through the

---

14   Not that this is saying much: the *Louis S St-Laurent* is 40 years old, and one of only two Canadian icebreakers capable of escorting a ship safely throughout her 900-mile voyage.

Passage saved the company about $200,000 on canal tolls, crew and bunkering costs and resulted in a comfortable profit.[15]

Professor John Higginbotham from Carleton University and former Canadian Assistant Deputy Minister of Transport, expressed his opinion to CTV News in January 2014:

> *Now that Nordic Bulk Carriers has shown it's possible — and is acting on that information with more crossings other shippers are likely to follow suit. . . I think there's some Canadian companies that got scooped. I believe they only woke up to this development.*

No doubt Fednav will have been discussing the case of the *Nordic Orion* with some animation when considering how they are to make the most of their own fleet investment.

Canada has a fleet of just six ageing icebreakers, really not designed to escort merchant shipping through the Passage, and no deep-water port for ships in transit at all; as a result, it has announced plans to build a new fleet of icebreakers, and a deep-water port. But it has also announced plans to build a fleet of Arctic patrol warships.

By contrast, Russia has all the experience necessary to forge ahead, thanks to its experience with the development of the Northern Sea Route. After the Russian revolution, Lenin ordered the development of the route, which, at first, was to serve the Soviet Union's Siberian settlements, which were mining coal and minerals for the country's industry; but the route later served as a crucial part of the supply chain in the war against Germany, in what the Russians call the Great Patriotic War.

The Soviets expanded their ability to serve the route when they launched a fleet of nuclear-powered icebreakers, beginning with the *Lenin* in 1957. The ships were expensive to build and operate, but they aided the Soviet Union in moving supplies throughout the nation's vast military–industrial complex in Siberia. During the Cold War, foreign ships were forbidden entry to the route which, at its peak in the 1980s, was carrying 6.6 million tonnes of cargo.

The rebirth of modern Russia saw the mass redundancy of its former military capability but, in recent years, Russia made progress toward rebuilding the route in order to exploit its global maritime opportunities in the era of global warming. In addition, unlike Canada, Russia has an impressive fleet of 37 icebreakers, including the only four nuclear-powered icebreakers in the world and, although they are an ageing population, Putin has led a drive for a new building

---

15 See: www.ctvnews.ca/business/danish-shipper-plans-more-commercial-travel-in-northwest-passage-1.1616200#ixzz2qSSYJW7w.

programme, with ships designed to cut through thicker ice and extend the navigation season. On 5 November 2013, the Kremlin's mouthpiece, Russia Today, reported that Russian shipbuilders are building a nuclear-powered mega icebreaker that will be able to cut through Arctic ice at any time of the year. It will be used to collect data along the continental shelf, but also *'further increase Russia's dominance in the region'*. In support of the risk–management function, Russia has also announced the reopening of a Soviet-era military base and airfield on the Novosibirsk Islands to provide greater safety and security, to *'make it possible for the emergency services, hydrologists, and climate specialists to work together to ensure the security and effective work of the Northern Sea Route'*.[16]

By comparison, there are no such facilities along the Northwest Passage at all.

Naturally, the master must keep in balance all the factors that contribute to the marine adventure – they have that ultimate responsibility, as the flag state's representative and the owner's agent, to bring the vessel safely to her port of discharge, intact and on time. For all that, they are still Master Under God, which has been reinforced by SOLAS Chapter V (Reg 34–1):[17]

> *The Owner, the charterer, the company operating the ship as defined in regulation IX/1, or any other person shall not prevent or restrict the master of the ship from taking or executing any decision which, in the master's professional judgement, is necessary for safety of life at sea and protection of the marine environment.*

The owner, the charterer, and everybody else will be relying on the master, therefore, to bring the ship safely to port – whatever the Arctic throws at them. Captain Roberts was an experienced Arctic Pilot, in command of the *Chelan*, a 500 gross ton tug freighter – ancestor of today's anchor handling tug supply vessel. On 15 April 1954, *Chelan* left Skagway on Canada's Pacific coast and had reached open sea when she caught the full force of a sudden Arctic gale. The Coast Guard received a laconic message: *Sinking Abandoning Ship*, but when the rescue teams made it to her location, they could discover nothing at all – the storm had left nothing to rescue. The Coast Guard concluded that the *Chelan* had been thrown sideways by a giant back-swell and speared on a rocky pinnacle.[18]

16 See http://news.nationalgeographic.com/news/energy/2013/11/131129-arctic-shipping-soars-led-by-russia/.

17 Brought into force under English domestic (flag and port state) law by the Merchant Shipping (Safety of Navigation) (Amendment) Regulations 2011.

18 Thanks to the late Captain Hamish Roberts for use of his family records.

The normative ethics of society have evolved another conventional standard of risk that appears to have overtaken the hazards to seafarers in the proprieties of coastal states. Given the underpinning importance of public perception, Roger Howard puts this context in his book *The Arctic Gold Rush*, when he identifies part of the problem in how people see the Arctic:[19]

> . . . *like any other wilderness, untouched and unspoilt by the hand of progress and civilization, but once lost, environmentalists point out, something unique and special can simply never be recovered.*

Merchant shipping operations present two specific environmental risks to the Arctic: the risk of damage caused as a result of a ship polluting the environment in transit, and the risk of consequences to the pristine environment caused by the extraction process, up to the point of crossing the ship's rail. The case of the *Exxon Valdez* illustrates the coastal state's response to the former; the *Deepwater Horizon* spill the latter. At least communication was efficient in both cases; but the High Arctic is on the very edge of the Inmarsat boundary, so that, even in fair weather, efficient response management is subject to inconsistent satellite service; in an Arctic blizzard the communication problem could be far worse. When confronted with the sort of weather that Captain Roberts faced, rescue and environmental protection in 2014 would be just as hazardous as it was in 1954. The scientific journal *Nature* reported that, at the height of the season for shipping movements, in August 2012, '*an unusually large and intense storm barrelled into the Arctic from Siberia*'.[20] It was described as a cyclone, raging for nearly two weeks and throwing about the ice in its midst. Against such natural forces, no stricken ship could survive and no rescue services could leave their own refuges, let alone mobilise the anti-pollution response that had been prepared in contingency plans. Moreover, meteorologists, climatologists and hydrologists construct the world's weather models on statistics to determine the likelihood of intense storms, oddly paying scant attention to the unexpected; while the effect of global warming has increased the number of unexpected extreme weather events at an alarming rate. Mercifully, there has not been a casualty in recent years to equal the *Chelan* disaster; yet, the increasing number of movements in the High Arctic has already led to a number of incidents in the Northern Sea Route, which demonstrate that a disaster is not a remote risk.

At the height of the Arctic shipping season in the summer of 2010, two Russian-flag tankers owned by the Murmansk Shipping Company, *Indiga* and *Varzuga*,

19 Howard, R, 2009, The Arctic Gold Rush, Continuum UK, London, p121.
20 Morello, L, 2013, 'Summer storms bolster Arctic ice', *Nature News*, Vol 500, 7464, Nature Publishing Group.

sailed from Murmansk loaded with 13,300 tonnes of diesel fuel; according to the passage plan, *Indiga* and *Varzuga* were scheduled to arrive in the port of Pevek in Russia's far east on 27 July. The *Indiga* was built in 1976, with a deadweight tonnage of 16,168, while the *Varzuga* was built a year later, capable of lifting a shade less tonnage of crude; both were designed for Arctic operations, however, with double hulls and ice-classification 1A Super. During the night of 16–17 July, the tankers were sailing through the partly ice-covered Northern Sea Route accompanied by two nuclear-powered icebreakers, *Rossia* and *Taimyr*, when the *Varzuga* crashed into the stern of the *Indiga*. The Russian port state authorities declined to give the exact position, but reported that they collided in difficult ice conditions, exacerbated by poor visibility. The authorities further reported that *Indiga* suffered some hull damage but she was not rendered unseaworthy, and no spill was reported.[21] The Russian Sea and River Transport Agency has the power to investigate marine accidents but no report has been published concerning any investigation and, so, no more light can be shed on the incident.

But the commercial opportunities to exploit the Northern Sea Route proved too good to suppress. From the embryonic use of the Northern Sea Route in 2010, the year of the *Indiga* casualty, 71 cargo ships transited the Route in 2013, carrying 1.4 million tonnes of cargo, responding to Vladimir Putin's encouragement in 2011:

> *The shortest Route between Europe's largest markets and the Asia-Pacific region lie across the Arctic. . . . I want to stress the importance of the Northern Sea Route as an international transport artery that will rival traditional trade lanes in service fees, security, and quality.*

Successful passages by crude tankers have become almost routine, while the Chinese-flag *Yong Sheng* became the first container ship to complete the passage when she arrived in Rotterdam on 10 September 2013, on a voyage from the Far East that was nine days and 2,800 nautical miles shorter than the conventional voyage through the Suez Canal.[22]

What could possibly go wrong?

On 4 September 2013, the Russian-flag tanker *Nordvik*, 6,403 deadweight tonnes, was carrying a full cargo of diesel fuel, when she struck an ice floe in Matisen Strait, and started taking on water travelling the Northern Sea Route.

The vessel, built in 1985, was classed only to travel in non-Arctic seas in thin ice, but the Northern Sea Route Administration had given the vessel permission

---

21 See Barents Observer for a report: http://barentsobserver.com/en/sections/articles/arctic-oil-tankers-collided.
22 *National Geographic* op cit.

to sail in the Kara Sea and the Laptev Sea, two of the most northern seas. 475 gallons of diesel oil were transferred from the damaged tanker into another tanker, and the Russian Sea and River Transport Agency reported that had been no leakage from the vessel. But the incident aroused deep concern throughout the Arctic region. A Russian union spokesperson said the accident was an example of the need for more emergency response capacity in the region prior to allowing vessels to travel in the Arctic seas. The union's spokesman, Alexander Bodnya, stated:[23]

> *Yesterday's accident was a direct threat to the lives of sailors and the ecology of the Arctic. Vessels like that should not be sailing on the Northern Sea Route, simply because they are not capable of withstanding the ice conditions.*

The alarm was reflected internationally when Lieutenant Governor Mead Treadwell wrote to the *Alaska Dispatch*:

> *Russia and other nations' crude oil and product tankers now come through the Bering Strait, through waters that are a major food source for Alaskans and the world. They should have contingency plans and the support of an oil spill response organization in case of a problem. That is not cheap, but we have to find a way to make it happen.*

The Northern Sea Route Information Office hastened to allay immediate fears by reporting that the nuclear icebreakers *Taimyr* and *Vaigach* finished the pilotage of the tanker *Nordvik* to ice-free waters; but then defended the administration with an attack that fell squarely on the master:[24]

> *The Northern Sea Route Administration granted the vessel permission to sail in the Kara Sea and the Laptev Sea only in light ice conditions. The official data on the types of ice conditions is published on the web site of the NSR Administration. The captain of the vessel in violation of the permit's requirements entered the water area with medium ice conditions, where the vessel's ballast tank was damaged. . . . There was not any oil leakage.*

Given this comment from the Russian state administration, it is apparent that the master's responsibility will be a major factor in the assessment of who is to

---

23 Reported by Alaska Dispatch, 13 September 2013. See www.alaskadispatch.com/article/20130913/russian-tanker-loaded-diesel-fuel-collides-arctic-ice-floe.

24 The NSR Information Office is owned and operated by the Centre for High North Logistics, formed in June 2011 as a joint initiative between CHNL and Rosatomflot, with additional financial support coming from Norwegian Barents Secretariat; but the Northern Sea Route Administration is firmly established within the sovereignty of Russia, with its office in Moscow. See www.arctic-lio.com/.

be held accountable. Of course, the administration's position is quite correct: the master will be in the front line of accountability, but it is the threat of criminalisation for that accountability that creates such alarm in maritime circles. The threat was conceived with the *Exxon Valdez*, but the concept was merely embryonic in that case; the prosecution of the masters in the cases of the *Erika*,[25] the *Prestige*[26] and the *Hebei Spirit*[27] brings the criminalisation phenomenon to stark maturity. A fatal accident would aggravate a mere pollution event that would, without doubt, result in a case of corporate manslaughter against the operator of the vessel, and the involvement of a flag state that will be very anxious indeed to protect its convention rights.

The reason is clear to China in its recent review of opportunities on the Northern Sea Route, for the commercial advantages of the route outweigh the risk of Russian intervention in China's flag state rights. With melting icecaps accelerating the opening of new shipping routes and the exploration of oil, gas and mineral deposits in the Arctic, China has been eager to gain a foothold in the region. Though it has no territorial claims in the Arctic, China has been lobbying for permanent observer status on the eight-member Arctic Council in a bid to gain influence.

Another way into the Arctic, as Beijing sees it, is by showing presence. In 2012 the Chinese icebreaker *Xuelong*, also known under her Anglicised name *Snow Dragon*, with a 119-member team aboard, became the first Chinese polar expedition ship to sail the full length of the Northern Sea Route into the Barents Sea and, subsequently, she sailed a straight line from Iceland to the Bering Strait via the North Pole.[28] *Xuelong* returned to her home port of Shanghai after completing the country's fifth Arctic expedition, which set off from Qingdao in east China's Shandong Province on 2 July 2012.

The sting in the tail of this story was yet to follow, however. In the Antarctic summer of 2014, the *Xuelong* assisted in a seven-hour operation to rescue 52 people among 74 who had been in peril on the Russian vessel *Akademik Shekalskiy* – but then she got trapped in the ice herself, and an Australian icebreaker, the *Aurora Australis*, was sent to stand by in the nearest open water until disaster was averted.

---

25 The casualty event took place in 1999; the master was exonerated by the judgment in 2012. See *The Erika*, Judgment No 9934895010, Tribunal de Grande Instance de Paris, 16 January 2008; Judgment 30 March 2010 (unreported).

26 The casualty event took place in 2002; the master was (partially) acquitted in 2013. See *Apostolos Mangouras*, Tribunal Superior de Justicia de Galicia, Judgment 13 November 2013 (unreported).

27 The casualty event took place in 2007; the master's conviction for the main charge was quashed in 2009 (unreported, but see Central Maritime Safety Tribunal, Decision Junghaeshim No 2008–26, Marine pollution caused by the collision of *Samsung No 1* (barge), towed by tugboats *Samsung T-5* and *Samho T-3*, and M/V *Hebei Spirit* (oil tanker), Notice of Decision on 4 December 2008).

28 http://barentsobserver.com/en/arctic/chinese-icebreaker-concludes-arctic-voyage-27-09.

These are bold new frontiers in shipping, but the opportunity in managing operations in polar seas takes the risk of corporate accountability for fatal accidents to new, pulse-quickening levels. From the lessons learned in this work, the risk appraisals will put an ever-greater strain on the relationship between the owner and their master, whose professional skill and judgement could lead to criminal charges for which the company would be vicariously liable.

Perhaps, though, it was ever so. Eighty years ago, Captain Arthur Raymer, one of the founding fathers of the Honourable Company of Master Mariners in London and a senior member of the Board of Trade in Southampton, had this to say[29] of the one, unchanging feature of seafaring:

> *The acid test of the sea lies in a man's work. If he has stamina and courage; and in the case of the more responsible positions, training and intelligence, then he will overcome the age-old perils of the sea and flourish. If he lacks these qualities, neither pride nor privilege will avail him. . . . The age old perils still persist — they seem to be nullified by radio, navigational aids, international organisations and every kind of mechanical ingenuity. They have certainly transformed much of the sea life but if vigilance and care are relaxed, if the man made scientific aids fail, the old sea demons of storm, rock, shoal, ice and fire lie in wait to pounce. The loss of many well found ships gives the lie to the theory that science has taken danger out of the modern sailor's life.*

Says it all.

---

29 Thanks to the late Molly Raymer for her permission to quote from her late father's unpublished papers.

Bibliographical sources

ACIA, 2005, 'Arctic Climate Impact Assessment – Scientific Report', Cambridge University Press, Cambridge

Allen, C K, 1931, *Legal Duties and other Essays in Jurisprudence*, The Clarendon Press, Oxford

Anon, 2007, *A Guide to the Corporate Manslaughter and Corporate Homicide Act 2007*, Ministry of Justice, London

Anon, 2007, *Corporate Manslaughter and Corporate Homicide Act 2007 – Explanatory Notes*, HMSO, London

Anon, 2010, *Corporate Manslaughter & Health and Safety Offences Causing Death – Definitive Guideline*, Sentencing Guidelines Council, London

Anon, 2012, 'Just Culture Policy, European Organisation for the Safety of Air Navigation (ERURONTROL)'. See e-sources

Anon, 2015, 'Sentencing Guidelines Secretariat, London. Effective from 1st February 2016'. See e-sources

ATSB Investigation number: 322-MO-2015–005 (Sanki Pacific)

Bauman, Z, 1987, *Legislators and Interpreters: On Modernity, Post-Modernity and Intellectuals*, Polity Press, Cambridge

Bundesstelle für Flugunfalluntersuchung, Investigation Report AX001–1–2/02 May 2004. See e-sources

Butcher L, 2010, House of Commons Standard Note SN/BT/769

Clark, A, 1910, *The Clipper Ship Era*, G E Putnam's Sons, New York

Clarke, L J, 2001, *Thames Safety Inquiry: 'Marchioness' / 'Bowbelle' – Formal Investigation Under the Merchant Shipping Act 1995*, DETR, London

Daniels, S, 2012, 'The Criminalisation of the Ship's Master. A new approach for the new Millennium', PhD thesis

Dekker, S and T Hugh, 2014, 'A just culture after mid-Staffordshire', BMJ August 2014

Eason, C, *Lloyd's List*, 16 January 2012, Informa plc, London

Ericson, R and K Carrière, 1994, 'The Fragmentation of Criminology', in D Nelken (ed), *The Futures of Criminology*, Sage, London

The Erika, Judgment No.9934895010, Tribunal de Grande Instance de Paris, 16 January 2008; Judgment 30 March 2010 (unreported)

Esler D et al, 2010, *Cytochrome P4501A biomarker indication of oil exposure in harlequin ducks up to 20 years after the Exxon Valdez oil spill. Environmental Toxicology and Chemistry*, Rice University, Houston

Gold, Professor E, 'The Protection of Masters and Seafarers from Criminalization: Emerging Problems for the Shipping Industry', Centre for Maritime Law, University of Queensland, Brisbane Prepared for the 31st Annual Conference 'Navigating the Sea of Change' The

Maritime Law Association of Australia and New Zealand Adelaide, South Australia 29 September – 1 October 2004

Home Office, 'Reforming the Law on Involuntary Manslaughter: The Government's Proposals' (Home Office, May, 2000, CC NO77828)

Home Office, 'Corporate Manslaughter: The Government's Draft Bill for Reform', Cm 6497, March 2005

'Home Affairs and Work and Pensions' – First Report, Session 2005–06, December 2005

Howard, R, 2009, *The Arctic Gold Rush*, Continuum UK, London, p121

Hudson, B, 2003, *Justice in the Risk Society*, Sage, London

Kolstad, J, 1990, *Report Ref M-90–26 through 31*, National Transportation Safety Board, Washington DC

Law Commission, 2010, *Criminal Liability in Regulatory Contexts*, Consultation Paper No 195, HMG, London

Lubbock, B, 1914, *The China Clippers*, Brown Son & Ferguson Ltd

Lyon, J, 1962, *Clipper Ships and Captains*, American Heritage Publishing, New York

MAIB, 1912, *British Wreck Commissioner's Inquiry, Report on the Loss of the 'Titanic' (SS)*

MAIB, 1987, *MV Herald of Free Enterprise. Report of Court No. 8074. Formal Investigation (July 1987)*

MAIB, 1989, *Report into the collision between the passenger Launch Marchioness and MV Bowbelle*

MAIB, 1990, *Report of the Chief Inspector of Marine Accidents into the collision between the passenger launch Marchioness and MV Bowbelle*

MacGregor, D, 1952, *The Tea Clippers*, Conway Maritime Press and Lloyd's of London Press

McCluskey, D, 2011, *The Law Society's Gazette*, The Law Society, London

Mateou, A and S Michaelides-Mateou, 2010, *Flying in the Face of Criminalization: The Safety Implications of Prosecuting Aviation Professionals for Accidents*, see e-sources

Ministry of Infrastructures and Transports Marine Casualties Investigative Body Cruise Ship Costa Concordia Marine casualty on January 13, 2012 Report on the safety technical investigation

Morello, L, 2013, 'Summer storms bolster Arctic ice', *Nature News*, Vol 500, 7464, Nature Publishing Group

Mukherjee, P, 2006, *Criminalisation and Unfair Treatment: The seafarer's Perspective*, see e-sources

Murphy, J, 2012, *Street on Torts*, 13th ed, Oxford University Press, Oxford

Nemsick, J and S Passeri, 2012, Criminalizing Aviation: Placing Blame Before Safety, accessed via http://apps.americanbar.org/litigation/committees/masstorts/articles/winter2012-criminalizing-aviation-blame-safety.html ©2012 by the American Bar Association. Reprinted With permission. All rights reserved. This information or any or portion thereof may not be copied or disseminated in any form or by any means or stored in an electronic database or retrieval system without the express written consent of the American Bar Association.

Ormerod, D, 2008, *Smith & Hogan Criminal Law*, Oxford University Press, Oxford

Richardson, P (ed), 2009, *Archbold Criminal Pleading, Evidence and Practice*, Thomson Reuters (Legal) Limited, London

Ruitenberg, B, 2002, 'Court case against Dutch Air Traffic Controllers', International Federation of Air Traffic Controllers' Associations, and LVNL, Amsterdam

Sale R and E Potatov, 2010, *The Scramble For The Arctic*, Frances Lincoln, London

Snook, S, 2000, *Friendly Fire: the accidental shootdown of US Black hawks over northern Iraq*, Princeton University Press, Princeton NJ

Swift, T, *Business Ethics: A European Review*, Vol 10, No 1, January 2001, Blackwell Publishers Ltd, London

Tadros, V, (2006), 'The Homicide Ladder', 69(4) MLR 601–618

Transcript of the Eighth Cadwallader Annual Memorial Lecture, 'The Extra-Territorial Jurisdiction in Criminalisation Cases: Sovereign Rights in Legislation and New Risks for the Shipping Industry', 2005, The London Shipping Law Centre, UCL, London

Transcript of Remarks and Replies to Media Questions by Russian Minister of Foreign Affairs Sergey Lavrov at Joint Press Conference with Philippine Foreign Affairs Secretary Alberto Romulo, Manila, 3 August 2007, Ministry of Foreign Affairs of the Russian Federation, Moscow

Trögeler, M, 2010, 'Criminalisation of air accidents and the creation of a Just Culture', accessed via http://media.leidenuniv.nl/legacy/mildred-tr-366geler-eala-prize.doc%29.pdf

E-Sources

Alaska Dispatch: www.alaskadispatch.com/article/20130913/russian-tanker-loaded-diesel-fuel-collides-arctic-ice-floe

Arctic North Sea Route Information Office: www.arctic-lio.com/

Barents Observer: www.barentsobserver.com/en/sections/articles/arctic-oil-tankers-collided

The Boeing Company 737 Technical site: www.b737.org.uk/accident_reports.htm

Bundesstelle für Flugunfalluntersuchung, Investigation Report AX001–1–2/02 May 2004: www.cfapp.icao.int/fsix/sr/reports/02001351_final_report_01.pdf

Eurocontrol: www.eurocontrol.int

Intertanko: www.intertanko.com

Jane's: www.janes.com/article/31525/russia-accelerates-arctic-militarisation

Kennedys Law LLP www.kennedyslaw.com/files/Uploads/Documents/Health%20and%20Safety/Kennedys%20-%20Defending%20corporate%20manslaughter.pdf

National Geographic: www.nationalgeographic.com/magazine/2016/03/new-arctic-thawing-rapidly-circle-work-oil/

National Snow and Ice Data Center: www.nsidc.org/arcticseaicenews/

Mateou, A and S Michaelides-Mateou, 2010, 'Flying in the Face of Criminalization: The Safety Implications of Prosecuting Aviation Professionals for Accidents': www.ashgate.com/isbn/9781409407676

Nemsick, J and S Passeri, 2012, 'Criminalizing Aviation: Placing Blame Before Safety': www.apps.americanbar.org/litigation/committees/masstorts/articles/winter2012-criminalizing-aviation-blame-safety.html

R v J M W Farm Limited, Belfast Crown Court Summary Judgment: www.courtsni.gov.uk/en-GB/Judicial%20Decisions/SummaryJudgments/Documents/Summary%20of%20judgment%20-%20R%20v%20J%20M%20W%20Farm%20Limited/j_sj_R-v-JMW-Farm-Limited_080512.pdf

Trögeler, M, 2010, 'Criminalisation of air accidents and the creation of a Just Culture': www.media.leidenuniv.nl/legacy/mildred-tr-366geler-eala-prize.doc%29.pdf

NTSB, www.ntsb.gov/news/events/Pages/Attempted_Takeoff_from_Wrong_Runway_Comair_Flight_5191_Bombardier_CL-600–2B19_N431CA_Lexington_Kentucky_August_27_2006.aspx

NTSB, www.ntsb.gov/news/press-releases/Pages/Update_on_NTSB_Investigation_into_the_Crash_of_Comair_Flight_5191.aspx

Sentencing Council: www.sentencingcouncil.org.uk/wp-content/uploads/HS-offences-definitive-guideline-FINAL-web.pdf

Swire Group: www.swire.com/en/our-businesses/marine-services/shipping-lines/swire-bulk

Index

Printed in Great Britain
by Amazon

28268893R00097